Young Person's Guide to UFOs

D1810822

Brian Ball

Young Person's Guide to UFOs

A UFO Spotters' guide

A DRAGON BOOK

GRANADA
London Toronto Sydney New York

Published by Granada Publishing Limited in 1979
Reprinted in 1980

ISBN 0 583 30292 0

A Dragon Original
Copyright © Brian Ball 1979

Granada Publishing Limited
Frogmore, St Albans, Herts AL2 2NF
and
3 Upper James Street, London W1R 4BP
866 United Nations Plaza, New York, NY 10017, USA
117 York Street, Sydney, NSW 2000, Australia
100 Skyway Avenue, Rexdale, Ontario, M9W 3A6, Canada
PO Box 84165, Greenside, 2034 Johannesburg, South Africa
61 Beach Road, Auckland, New Zealand

Set, printed and bound in Great Britain by
Cox & Wyman Ltd, Reading
Set in Intertype Times

*This book is dedicated to Chris, Nick and Jeremy;
and to Rolf too.*

Contents

Acknowledgements

I have to thank the members of ISTRA (the Interplanetary Space Travel Research Association) and BUFORA (the British Unidentified Flying Object Research Association) who helped in researching this book. Norman Oliver, Editor the BUFORA Journal kindly gave me permission to quote from his article about Sergeant Cockcroft's sighting of a UFO during the Second World War (the article first appeared in September/October 1977 in the Journal). Betty Wood of BUFORA was an enthusiastic correspondent, and I am especially indebted to Mike Parry, Honorary President of ISTRA, for his invaluable assistance and also for giving permission to reprint the UFO questionnaire in Chapter 8 of this work.

Chapter One

UFOs and Flying Saucers

When does a UFO stop being a UFO?

It's not a trick question. The answer is that an Unidentified Flying Object stops being a UFO the moment it is identified – and then it's an IFO, an Identified Flying Object. Many of the reports of flying objects have later turned out to be fairly ordinary things, like weather balloons or the landing lights of an aircraft. But many sightings haven't been explained – and they're still UFOs.

But how did UFOs come to be called *flying saucers*?

To answer that question we have to go back to June 1947, when an American civilian pilot called Kenneth Arnold joined in the search for a missing aircraft. All pilots in the area had been requested to watch out for the wreckage of a Marine Transport plane thought to have come down in the mountains. The sky was clear and visibility was excellent. At two o'clock in the afternoon, Mr Arnold was flying at around nine thousand feet near Mount Rainier in the Rocky Mountains when below him he saw a flash of bright light.

And then a whole series of bright lights.

There were nine of them, flying in and out of the peaks with a dipping, zig-zagging movement. Their size was about fifty feet across – about the length and width of a 1940s medium-sized aircraft. But they didn't look like any plane Mr Arnold had seen.

They looked like saucers.

'They looked like *what*?' a reporter asked him later, when he was interviewed about the mysterious discs.

So Mr Arnold explained that he had seen nine silvery disc-shaped objects flying in formation below him, and that they seemed to be skipping along in the kind of flight you would expect if you skimmed a round flat stone on water.

They were moving faster than any aircraft he had ever seen, and they had the shape of saucers.

The newsmen were fascinated. They wanted to know if the strange objects had wings.

'No,' said Mr Arnold. 'No wings.'

But how did the silvery discs manage to fly? the news reporters asked. What kind of engines powered them?

'I don't know,' said Mr Arnold.

Mr Arnold hadn't seen any engines. The objects were discs, not at all the usual shape of an aircraft – and there were no wings, no tailplane, no engines.

'So they weren't aircraft?'

'I don't know what they were,' said Mr Arnold.

'And there were nine of them?'

'Yes, nine.'

'Nine shining lights, You really saw them, sir?'

So Mr Arnold went over it all again. He had seen a flash of light first, then the discs skipping along like saucers.

'Like saucers flying?' said one newsman. 'Is that what you saw?'

'Like flying saucers?' said another news reporter. '*Flying saucers!*'

Mr Arnold's story of mysterious shining discs flying in and out of peaks was soon being talked about all over America, and then all over the world. What were *flying saucers*?

People immediately wanted to know more about them. And, since it's the job of newsmen to produce stories that people want to read, every new sighting of a strange object in the sky became a flying-saucer story.

When an American warplane pilot tried to chase a lighted UFO one night in 1948, the story that was made out of the incident became DOG-FIGHT WITH FLYING SAUCER! and F-51 BATTLES WITH SAUCER!

It happened in October 1948. The pilot was Lieutenant George Gorman, who had been out on a practice flight and was returning to his base at Fargo, North Dakota, USA. He was an experienced fighter-pilot, and when he saw a fast-moving white light over his base he turned his F-51 warplane north to intercept it. The speeding object was disc-shaped!

Ground-staff watched.

Lieutenant Gorman threw the plane about the sky again and again, but the mysterious object managed to evade him each time he approached it. The watchers were sure he was engaged in a genuine dog-fight, and so was Lieutenant Gorman.

Was it a flying saucer?

The newscasters thought so.

'No,' said the meteorologists who recognized Lieutenant Gorman's UFO from its description.

'Are you sure?' demanded Lieutenant Gorman's superiors, who were very touchy about UFOs entering American air space.

'We'll show you how to make one just like it,' the meteorologists said. And they did. They demonstrated with a large balloon and reproduced Lieutenant Gorman's UFO.

There were plenty of sightings which could not be explained so easily. And the name *flying saucers* stuck. Ships' officers reported seeing flying saucers at sea. Weathermen in the Arctic and the Antarctic spotted flying saucers. They were seen by policemen on patrol, and by thousands of ordinary men, women and children. And there were many sightings by the commercial pilots, who spent their working days and nights at the controls of high-flying jet aircraft, and who were trained to be on constant alert for unusual happenings in the skies. One such pilot saw UFOs over Labrador.

Captain James Howard was piloting the BOAC Stratocruiser *Centaurus* on the night of 29 June 1954 when he saw a whole flight of UFOs. 'Do you see *that*!' he said to his First Officer.

Dawn was just breaking, but visibility was poor. First Officer Lee Boyd and the navigating officer saw the UFOs too – a large craft with several smaller ones around it. At first they thought they were being tracked by hostile aircraft. It was the time of the Cold War, when the United States and the USSR kept huge fleets of fighter planes and bombers on constant patrol to guard against violations of their air space.

11

Were these some new kind of military aircraft?

'Check with Goose Bay,' ordered Captain Howard.

At Goose Bay, Labrador, in the far north of the American continent, the United States Air Force kept jet-interceptors ready to counter any threats. Commanders were ordered to investigate at once any mysterious objects in the skies.

In the hazy skies, the UFOs maintained a course parallel to the *Centaurus*. The Goose Bay commander asked for a description of the intruders.

'There's a huge pear-shaped craft with a number of smaller cones,' Captain Howard reported.

A jet-interceptor streaked into the sky to investigate.

Aboard the *Centaurus* the crew watched in amazement and apprehension as the big UFO closed on them. At first they had not been able to make out its shape, but they could see that it was not a disc, like the smaller craft. It was huge – as big as an ocean liner.

'It's closing,' reported Captain Howard.

The pilot of the interceptor asked for more information, but the crew could tell him little. All they could make out was a vast, hazy shape.

For a quarter of an hour, the UFO and its attendant craft matched speed with the big passenger airliner. Captain Howard had the impression that the *Centaurus* was under observation now.

'Interceptor near your air space,' reported ground control at Goose Bay. 'You should see it soon.'

But the fighter plane was too late.

Captain Howard saw the monster object suddenly accelerate and hurtle away at a tremendous speed. By the time the pilot of the jet-interceptor was in sight of the *Centaurus*, the UFO had vanished.

'And the smaller craft? Captain Howard was asked, when he made his report. He hadn't seen them once the big UFO closed, but the navigating officer thought they had gone inside it.

'And what were the UFOs doing?' asked reporters. Captain Howard suggested that they could have been extraterrestrial craft on a reconnaissance mission. But why they should choose his Stratocruiser for their inspection was beyond him.

It was much the same story with other UFOs. They were sighted, they were chased, they were photographed, and though many turned out to be hoaxes or IFOs, others remained fascinatingly mysterious.

Were they flying saucers?

Some pilots began to remember seeing mysterious flying objects during their wartime years, like the UFO seen by the crew of a bomber one night in May 1943.

Sergeant Cockcroft was aboard a British Halifax bomber based near York. The Halifax set out with a force of five hundred aircraft to attack the Krupps Armaments Works at Essen, Germany. There were seven men in the crew: two gunners, a navigator, a bomb aimer, a flight engineer, pilot and second pilot.

There were plenty of dangers for the Halifax. Flak burst around the aircraft as it crossed the Dutch coast, and the rear gunner engaged a German night-fighter. Brilliant trails of tracer flared in the night sky as the JU88 attacked the British bomber, which was hit several times, but its return fire drove the attacker away.

The flak in the Ruhr Valley was worse. Air-bursts of exploding metal casings brought down bomber after bomber, but the Halifax flew steadily on to the brilliantly lit target, where a flight of bombers had already dropped their loads of explosives and incendiaries on the munitions works.

It was just before the Captain lined up the bomber for the run-in to the target that the UFO was first sighted – and it was the Captain who saw it first.

'Port – bandit on port side!' he called.

The mid-upper gunner and the rest of the crew were alerted, but this was no hostile aircraft. It was hanging in the sky at the same height as the Halifax and, as with so many sightings of UFOs, it was like no aircraft the observers had seen before.

It was bigger altogether than the Halifax, and silvery gold in colour. The shape was cylindrical. Along the silver-gold

13

length of the UFO was a series of what looked like port-holes.

'What *is* it?' the crew members wanted to know.

'What's it doing there?' asked Sergeant Cockcroft.

The Captain and those of his crew who could see the UFO were completely baffled. They were only a minute or so from their run-in to the blazing target 18,000 feet below, and they were flying through all the flak the German defences could throw at them.

There was no time to speculate on the nature of the weird object hovering near them. The Captain turned his plane to follow the first wave of heavy bombers as the amazed crew members were calling to one another about the UFO. There was no time to worry about it, not then. Getting safely back to base was the first priority.

Years later, Sergeant Cockcroft told his story. 'I think that the first reaction of most of us was amazement because this object just had no right to be there. After a very short space of time, twenty or thirty seconds, it suddenly began moving and, retaining its altitude, climbed away, acceler-ating extremely rapidly until it vanished from sight. The speed it attained seemed to us, in those days, completely incredible. It was certainly into the thousands of miles an hour. As it accelerated, the outline became blurred and the shape foreshortened. The size is more difficult to judge, but it was very large, certainly very much bigger than our own aircraft, appearing at least as long as a king-sized cigarette or small cigar at arm's length. We then completed our bomb run and returned to base.'

This is another case of an unidentified craft able to fly far faster than aircraft of the time. Naturally, it was reported to the Intelligence Officer at the Bomber Command base, but there didn't seem to be any special interest in it – one more unusual sighting which didn't happen to be an enemy craft wasn't an important matter in wartime.

Was this a flying saucer?

Sergeant Cockcroft said this: 'I have never seen anything of this nature before or since, and have never seen any of the saucer-shaped objects, but in retrospect I am quite convinced that this cigar-shaped UFO was of extra-terrestrial origin. Although it happened a long time ago, the sighting was by a group of experts, none of whom could offer any rational explanation.'

Yet though many people were convinced that flying saucers were alien space-ships, no one had been able to prove they were.

The few photographs taken of UFOs weren't much help.

A lady in South Africa who claimed to know that UFOs were flying saucers produced three photographs of disc-shaped objects. They looked like some kind of flying objects, and several newspapers published the photographs as pictures of flying saucers.

Were they?

Experts looked closely at the prints. 'Hub caps,' they decided. 'They look like automobile hub-caps.'

Not many people had a camera with them when they spotted a UFO, but Warrant Officer Newhouse of the US Navy did. He took a movie film of a number of flying saucers in 1952.

Mrs Newhouse spotted the flying saucers first. They were driving with their children near Tremonton, Utah, when Mrs Newhouse saw a flight of shining UFOs in the east. Mr Newhouse stopped the car and grabbed his movie camera, for 1952 was a time when there was tremendous interest in UFOs. He knew how valuable a movie film would be. Carefully he adjusted the telephoto lens of his camera and tracked the UFOs as they crossed the clear Utah sky. Then he kept the camera still and took a film of one of the UFOs, letting it cross the lens.

When the film was developed, it seemed that he had proved that flying saucers had invaded United States air space. Mr Newhouse had taken the best shots of UFOs up to that time.

The film was at once passed on to Navy and Air Force experts.

Could Mr Newhouse's film solve the mystery of the flying saucers?

When the photographic experts made their report, they

were questioned by members of a committee which had been set up to decide if UFOs were a threat to the United States. *Were they a threat?*

'Not these UFOs,' said one expert. 'Seagulls aren't going to provide much opposition for the Air Force.'

'Seagulls!' another said. 'These are flying saucers. Whoever heard of seagulls flying at a thousand miles an hour. That's what these flying saucers are doing in this film!'

Other experts weren't so decided in their opinions.

'I have examined the film, and all I can tell you is that they are self-luminous objects which I cannot identify. There's nothing else on the film to show how big they are or how fast they're moving.'

'Agreed,' said another. 'If the objects in the film were ten miles from the camera, then the speed indicated is a thousand miles an hour. But there is no way of telling from the frames I have seen just how far Mr Newhouse was from the light-sources.'

The 1952 investigation showed that the UFOs in Mr Newhouse's film weren't aircraft.

But what were they?

One of the investigating team of experts was in agreement with many members of the American public when he said that he believed that they were alien space-ships. The film was examined again some years later, though, and the panel of experts who reported back said: 'The way the light catches a flock of seagulls would produce an effect similar to that in the film taken at Tremonton, Utah, in 1952.'

Even the best-authenticated photographs and movie pictures couldn't provide an answer to the mystery of the fast-moving unidentified flying objects. Pictures proved that *something* had crossed the skies, but gave no explanation of that *something*.

Sightings were reported all over the world. UFOs could be hundreds of feet across, or no larger than a dinner-plate. Most, though, seemed to be around the size of a small modern aircraft. They came in many shapes and colours. Some glowed, like a sun, while many were palely luminous.

The disc shape was the type most often seen, with some variations.

'It was shaped like a World War I helmet,' said one Australian UFO-spotter, while the UFO seen by a pilot at Le Bourget Airport was egg-shaped.

'The flying saucer had much the appearance of the planet Saturn,' explained one lady who saw a UFO one night in 1956. 'There were two flattened half-spheres and a rim separating them.'

And UFOs were described as looking like mushrooms, diamond-edged discs, and tear drops. They could be red, orange, yellow, green, blue and purple – all these colours were reported.

There were reports of whole formations of flying saucers, though most informants saw only one at a time. Quite a few reports mentioned a parent craft with numbers of smaller UFOs, like the sighting by Captain Howard.

And what powered the flying saucers?

Most of them were seen to travel at tremendous speeds, but only rarely did a witness see any kind of power-source. Some were rocket-propelled, but not many. There was usually a whining noise, or a *whoosh*! when the flying saucer took off, otherwise they travelled silently.

There were so many reports – thousands of them – of bizarre happenings in the skies that many people refused to accept the results of government inquiries which announced that flying saucers did not exist.

'There are scores of perfectly ordinary occurrences that could *look* like flying saucers,' explained scientists who advised the American government. 'They could be anything from weather balloons to comets. People see what they *think* they see, and just now everyone's heard so much about flying saucers they get mixed up. In a little while, the UFO craze will die down.'

This was in the 1950s.

Chapter Two

Flying Saucer Invaders?

By the early 1950s there was serious talk about alien invasion by flying saucers. The idea wasn't new. H. G. Wells' 1901 novel *The War of the Worlds* was broadcast as a radio play in 1938.

'Monster tripods with death-rays are advancing,' announced a newscaster. 'The Martians are destroying all before them!'

People panicked, for they believed that it was a real news bulletin, not a radio drama. They grabbed guns and food and headed away from the cities. There was panic for several hours, until the authorities managed to convince them that it was fiction, not fact.

There had been other stories of Martian invasion, too.

In the period 1896–7, there were newspaper stories of gigantic airships appearing in the skies over America. Sometimes they landed, and their crews explained that they had come from Venus or Mars. Most of the stories were hoaxes, but in the 1950s they were remembered by the older generations.

Could this be another invasion by space-craft?

Many Americans thought so, especially when it seemed that the capital of the United States was under observation by mysterious unidentified flying objects!

It was the time known to UFO investigators as the '1952 Flap'.

Through the summer of 1952, whole formations of flying saucers were spotted in various parts of the USA. During the previous five years, many individual sightings had been reported, but not on this scale.

When the flying saucers seemed to concentrate on targets of national security, such as the headquarters of the Air

18

Defence System at Andrews Air Force Base, the secret Atomic Energy Commission Laboratories, and Washington Airport, there was consternation amongst sections of the American public.

The flying saucers were spotted singly, in groups, and in formations. They hovered, just as other UFOs had done, and then accelerated at speeds up to seven thousand miles an hour.

Radar operators checked their sets and found that they were reporting accurately. The invaders were able to manoeuvre at tremendous speeds, far in excess of anything the American Air Force could send up.

Airline pilots and passengers watched the flying saucers. There were several reports that confirmed the presence of white lights moving at great speed over the nation's capital city.

One daylight sighting was reported and tracked by radar until the intruder could be intercepted by a jet fighter. The pilot was vectored in on to the UFO, but after sighting it he could not match its speed. He chased it after it was spotted over the highly secret nuclear station near Washington, but he could not get close enough to make a firm identification.

Again and again mysterious white lights were reported by day and by night, and as many as ten blips at a time appeared on radar screens.

The Air Force was alarmed.

Towards the end of July, there were reports of flying saucers making a night reconnaissance over the White House itself.

F-94 night-fighters went up to intercept. The interceptors soon found the mysterious white lights and searched the area for three hours. But, once again, except in one case, the UFOs evaded them: Lieutenant William Patterson's flight heard him say that he had not only located the UFOs, they had surrounded him! There were four of them, keeping pace with his F-94, two on each side. When he tried to manoeuvre, they sped away, and that was the last he saw of them.

It was very unsatisfactory.

19

Experienced pilots in the latest jets couldn't catch the flying saucers – if that is what they were. The radar operators could track the swerving, fast-moving objects but they couldn't properly identify them. But one military man could.

Major Kolman VonKevizky was sure that the UFOs were the spearhead of a galactic task force sent to observe the capital of the United States and report on the reaction to observation by space-craft.

What was his advice?

Prepare for a space war!

'Not against these intruders,' explained meteorological experts. 'These sightings aren't flying saucers. They're not UFOs. They're tricky, but they're harmless. Just the refraction of ground lights from unusual temperature layers.'

'How about that!' most of the Air Force jet pilots said. 'We've been chasing street-lights!'

'But how about the radar trackings?' argued the electronics experts. 'There were tracks of UFOs exactly where the lights were sighted.'

'Same thing,' explained the scientists. 'You'd get a radar bounce back from the hot and cold layers. Freaky, but natural.'

Major VonKevizky, of course, was not satisfied. He believed that the American public was being wilfully misinformed by the government. Well-paid scientists, he declared, were compelled to conceal the truth of the 'interstellar invasion'.

Major VonKevizky spoke of a 'cover-up'.

Many Americans shared his opinions. They wouldn't accept that the mysterious lights were street-lights and car headlights, as experts had explained. To them, it was clear that the Air Force had identified the intruders as aliens, and that the American government was scared of saying so.

It's easy to see how the American public was confused. There were reports of the UFOs in newspapers, on radio, on TV programmes and in magazines. Photographs showed flying saucers over the White House. Famous politicians and military leaders were sought out and interviewed – and some of them said they weren't sure of what was happening.

In 1938 the radio broadcast of *The War of the Worlds* had been enough to start a full-scale panic in America. And that was fiction. But here were *sightings* of what could be extra-terrestrials; sightings, radar tracks, and photographs.

What more proof could you ask?

That was the way many men and women reasoned. *Flying saucers were real.* They had to be!

And there were many people who believed that the flying saucers were hostile. They reasoned like this:

If the invaders from space were friendly, why didn't they make contact? By not making contact, they *proved* themselves to be unfriendly. Anyway, if they're so far in advance of us they make our fastest planes look like kids' kites, we're right to be scared of them.

Why wasn't the Air Force doing something?

It was. An inquiry known first as 'Project Sign' and then 'Project Grudge' had begun to make a detailed study of UFO reports soon after Mr Arnold's 1947 sighting. Investigating officers had reported that the UFOs were not a serious menace to the United States.

The 1952 Flap changed things. Flying saucers over the White House had to be taken seriously.

So 'Project Blue Book' was set up to record all UFO sightings, and scientists were called in to help. The United States government was as determined as the American public to solve the mystery of the UFOs.

About the same time, in the early 1950s, a number of private citizens claimed to have discovered the reason for the flying-saucer invasion. They were the 'contactees' – a name given to those who said they had been in contact with extra-terrestrials from flying saucers. If the American public wanted to know whether or not flying-saucer people were hostile, there were plenty of answers from the contactees.

'Definitely not,' said George Adamski, who wrote a book about his experiences. 'Flying-saucer people have nothing but goodwill towards Earthlings. They are not hostile.'

How did George Adamski know?

21

Because, so he explained, he had been contacted by the crew of a flying saucer.

He wasn't the only person to report a meeting with extra-terrestrials from flying saucers. Joe Simonton of Wisconsin, Missouri, found a flying saucer in his drive. He heard noises outside his farmhouse and looked out of a window. He was astonished to see a shining, silvery craft descending steadily on to his drive! It was about eleven o'clock in the morning.

'Then what?' asked a reporter.

'A kinda hatch opened,' said Mr Simonton. 'There were three guys inside and they started making signs at me. No words, just signs.'

'What kind of signs, Mr Simonton?'

Joe Simonton explained. One of the men held up a container like a large jug or a bucket, and indicated that he wanted it filled. So, obligingly, Mr Simonton filled it with water.

'I handed it to him and as I did he reached down and took it,' went on Mr Simonton. 'As I stepped back I looked up to the hatchway, and there was this man cooking these pancakes. So I pointed to him and made a gesture like eating. So the man who took the water reached over and took a handful of these pancakes and handed them to me. They were so hot and greasy I could hardly hold them. Then he closed the hatch with a click, and when he closed it you couldn't any more see where it shut than you could see a hole in my hand.'

'And that's when the UFO took off moving south?' the reporter asked.

'Yes, sir. It disappeared in three seconds and there was I left with a handful of hot greasy pancakes.'

Joe Simonton was a retired police officer, and so he became known in the United States as the 'Pancake Cop'. It made a cheerful story for the news media, though it was investigated by serious researchers. Though they found that Mr Simonton had always been known as a reliable and honest citizen, the idea of flying-saucer crews giving away pancakes made the story seem absurd, and it wasn't taken seriously by the authorities. Pancakes couldn't be much of a

22

threat to the United States, especially as after analysis they were found to be made of fairly ordinary ingredients – flour, salt and oil. *What did they taste like?*

'It was like chewing cardboard,' said Mr Simonton.

The UFO that called at the Wisconsin chicken farm caused amusement rather than alarm. If it couldn't be explained away like some of the other flying-saucer reports, it at least indicated that the crew wasn't hostile.

Another report of a mysterious flying craft came from an American priest, Father William B. Gill, who was in charge of a mission school at Boianai, Papua, New Guinea.

In the summer of 1959, Father Gill reported that he had seen what appeared to be human-like figures waving to him from UFOs. Though the sun had set, it was still quite light when the first UFOs were sighted. There was a 'mother ship', according to Father Gill, and a number of smaller craft.

Some of the members of the mission were with Father Gill, pupils as well as teachers. On various evenings, and sometimes in the early morning, there were strange occurrences.

A startling explosion woke up many of the people at Boianai one night, an ear-splitting noise too loud for thunder. Vivid bright lights were observed which changed colour from green to red. Father Gill, one Saturday night, counted as many as seven smaller UFOs together with a much larger parent craft.

'The mother ship is about thirty-five feet across,' he declared. 'It has a top deck that must be around twenty feet across. I estimate that it carries a crew of four men.'

This is the strangest part of the UFOs sighting. Not only did the UFOs remain in the area for a considerable period, they appeared to be willing to contact the members of the Boianai Station. For a quarter of an hour one June night, Father Gill and several others watched as the UFOs hovered above. Four men-like figures appeared to be setting up some kind of apparatus outside the dome which the observers below could not see. Father Gill waved to one of the figures.

'To my surprise,' he reports, 'the figure waved back.'

That was as far as the contact went. The men-like figures went back into the dome, but later two of them returned to carry on with what they were doing. Shortly afterwards, a blue spotlight came from the UFO.

Were they flying saucers?

'They were more like discs than saucers,' said Father Gill. And he drew them. The drawings showed an oval-shaped craft, with four spindly legs. The craft was domed, and on the dome Father Gill placed the four figures he had seen.

Were they a threat to Earth?

It didn't seem so, any more than were Mr Joe Simonton's visitors. In fact, one scientific explanation of the Papuan UFO sighting is that it was probably the planet Venus that Father Gill and his Papuan teachers and pupils saw. The planet was in the right place for observation during those summer evenings. And Venus sometimes does seem to change colour in the way that some of the observers describe – from white to red, and occasionally to green.

Will there be an invasion of Earth? That was the question that still worried many people, especially in the United States. *If these things are alien space-ships, will they attack us?*

'They are space-ships and they won't attack,' said Mr Adamski.

Mr George Adamski, who had been on the look-out for space-ships since the 1930s, wrote several books about his experiences with extra-terrestrials. 'They are benevolent,' he said. 'I *know*!' He claimed that in 1952 he was contacted by a Venusian.

Mr Adamski had originally come to the United States from Poland, and his main interest was astronomy. Years before the first flying-saucer stories were published, he was convinced that he had seen many UFOs, and that they were space-ships. In many lectures, magazine articles, and in his various books, Mr Adamski told of his feelings that something important was going to happen.

On the night of 20 November 1952 he and a number of his friends set out for a remote region of California to try to contact visitors from outer space. The investigators sighted a cigar-shaped craft and went to find where it had landed.

According to Mr Adamski, they didn't find the craft immediately. But they did see a strange-looking figure approaching them. He was dressed in flowing clothes, with a wide belt and thin sandals, and although he was otherwise human in appearance he seemed alien.

Mr Adamski would not allow his companions to endanger themselves by approaching the stranger. He told them to wait whilst he spoke to him.

'Where are you from?' asked Mr Adamski.

But the stranger could not speak English.

'Then how did you communicate with him?' newsmen asked.

'By telepathic means,' Mr Adamski said.

'You could read his thoughts?'

'I could read much of what was in his mind. We also communicated by using gestures.'

Mr Adamski explained. The stranger came from Venus. He had found this out by drawing a circle in the sand to represent the Sun, and then drawing more circles to show the positions of the solar system. To show that he came from Venus, the stranger pointed to the second circle outwards from the Sun. *Venus!*

'Then you saw the flying saucer, Mr Adamski?' he was asked.

'I saw it, yes.'

'Would you describe it for us?'

'It was round, with a dome. There were port-holes, I saw them distinctly. I'd say it was around thirty-five feet in diameter.'

'And what was its power source? Can you tell us?'

'I'm sure that some form of magnetic force provides the power unit for the Venusians' ships.'

But how about the cigar-shaped craft? Where had that gone?

Mr Adamski found out later in 1952. He wrote of his experiences in his book, *Inside the Space-Ships*. The cigar-shaped craft were the parent-ships, whilst the flying saucers were smaller, scout ships. The second time that he saw the

25

Venusian, Mr Adamski said he was asked to step inside the flying saucer. He did so, and he was whisked away into space to meet the extra-terrestrials who had chosen him to take their message to the people of Earth. They were beings from three planets, Venus, Saturn and Mars. Mr Adamski learned their names and their reason for visiting this planet, which was anything but a threat.

They sent their message: *We are a more advanced form of civilization than yours. We know the kind of dangers that threaten you. We come to warn you of them.*

Telepathy?

Flying saucers?

Warnings from outer space?

It sounded to many people like a science-fiction story.

But there were thousands of Americans, and others in various parts of the world, who believed every word that Mr Adamski had written. Groups were formed so that people could discuss his experiences and then themselves attempt to contact the extra-terrestrials.

In the 1950s there were scores of such groups of people who were fascinated by the idea of the visitors from beyond Earth. Even now, there are societies which hold to the truth of George Adamski's accounts of his experiences.

But did it all really happen?

Maybe. The mind can play tricks, so psychologists tell us. Maybe Mr Adamski's experiences happened in his own mind, not in outer space. It could be that he was subject to strange visions, perhaps of the kind that pass vividly through the mind during sleep as dreams, or as spectacular fantasies when we're in a feverish or drugged state.

In any event, the public was assured they had nothing to fear from Mr Adamski's space-men.

Mr Adamski took a number of photographs of the Venusian space-ship, but when they were developed it turned out that his camera had not been properly focused. All that came out was a blurred shape of a disc with a domed top.

When the photograph was reproduced in a book about his experiences, experts examined it.

Was it a Venusian scout-ship?

'It looks like a chicken brooder,' explained photographic experts.

'But there are the port-holes in the sides!' argued flying-saucer enthusiasts.

'Rivets,' said the experts.

Mr Adamski wasn't the only person to claim to have been in touch with extra-terrestrials who brought a message to the people of Earth.

A Californian bill-poster named Allen Noonan stated that he had been transported by some mysterious means to a place beyond Earth, where he was told that the invasion of our planet had already begun.

'Flying-saucer bases have already been established in the Earth,' he declared.

'*In* the Earth, Mr Noonan?' asked an interviewer. 'Don't you mean *on* the planet?'

'No.'

Mr Noonan explained. He declared that the space-men flew into their bases which were at the poles. Flying saucers flew down great openings to get to the interior of Earth, for Earth was hollow. Inside the planet was a central sun – and it was this sun shining from the openings at the north and south pole that caused the Northern Lights.

'And how do you communicate with these beings?' Mr Noonan was asked.

'By telepathy.'

That was Mr Noonan's story of his experiences.

Another American citizen who claimed to have encountered beings from beyond Earth was Mr Woodrow Derenberger.

'And how did you speak to them?' newsmen asked him.

It was telepathy again. Mr Derenberger's mind, so he learned, was in tune with the minds of beings from somewhere that sounded to him like 'The Galaxy of Genemedes'.

'And why are they here?' an interviewer asked Mr Derenberger.

'They're interested in trading with us,' he said.

It didn't seem that Mr Derenberger's aliens were a threat,

and nothing more was heard of the space-men Mr Noonan had seen.

There were more visits by extra-terrestrials, according to other contactees, most of them from planets of the solar system.

One expedition came from a planet invisible to us.

David Swanner, of Tennessee, USA, was contacted by beings who were rather smaller than humans – they were around two-thirds of our size. They came, so Mr Swanner reported, from a planet exactly opposite to us on the other side of the Sun which is why we are unable to see it.

Mr Swanner was told something of the history of the aliens. They were called Plantos, he said, and they had suffered the effects of atomic attack about half a century ago. Since then, they had built giant atomic engines to repel invasion. Again, though, Mr Swanner's aliens didn't intend any harm to Earth. They came in their flying saucers to help us.

There were more reports. People stated that they had experienced weird happenings whilst driving their cars along quiet roads. Engines had suddenly cut out, and then UFOs hovered above the stalled cars.

In Brazil a man and his wife believed that they had been picked up by a flying saucer – they were still in their car – and dropped safely a few moments later a hundred miles from their starting-point. But they were unharmed, and that seems to be one of the things we learn from all of those who have been in contact with the crews of UFOs – whatever they are, they're harmless.

Most people regarded the contactees as harmless themselves – harmless cranks. And of course the American Air Force showed little interest in their stories of flying-saucer aliens.

Chapter Three

Tracking the Intruders

Most sightings of UFOs are by people who haven't a camera handy to record what they've seen. And when photographs and movie films are taken, they are generally hazy and difficult to identify as anything more than fuzzy dots. Even when professional flyers like airline pilots see UFOs – and they're in the best place to observe them, miles up in the sky with a clear horizon in all directions – mostly they can't be sure as to exactly what they have seen.

UFOs have been spotted by many pilots, but few have been able to investigate them. The safety of the passengers comes first, and an airliner has to keep to its flight-path. Once, though, a pilot was able to give chase to an unidentified flying object. And he was in the ideal aircraft to track it.

At ten past ten on the morning of 17 July 1957 Major Chase of the United States Air Force glanced out of the starboard window of the RB-47 he was flying. He saw a UFO.

It was a brilliant flash of white light tinged with blue, and it was closing fast. At first he thought it was the kind of emergency which fliers dread above all others – another plane on a collision course.

'Landing lights! Airliner at eleven o'clock!' he called to his co-pilot, Captain McCord.

The six men of the crew heard and were alert at once. Major Chase tensed, ready to fling the Air Force jet out of the path of the airliner. The crew were already plotting the course of the closing aircraft. They were highly trained electronics personnel and this was their job.

The UFO registered on the radar-detection screens.

'Closing fast,' reported the operators.

It was a frightening moment.

29

Before Major Chase could change course, though, the brilliant light moved upwards and left of the RB-47 at a speed which seemed impossible. No aircraft could move that fast. Major Chase was an experienced pilot. He *knew* it could not have been a plane.

This incident might have been just another sighting of a strange object in the sky but for one thing: the RB-47. Major Chase and his six-man crew were out on a training mission from the Forbes Air Force Base at Topeka, in the Air Force's latest reconaissance plane, the RB-47.

It was crammed with detector equipment. Direction-finding electro-magnetic scanners covered the air space around the jet. They were not radar – they didn't send out a beam to locate planes. The scanners were designed to pick up the searching radar beams of other transmitters, so that they could be classified and identified. The RB-47 was built to home in on transmissions from intruders.

Before the UFO was sighted, Major Chase had taken the Air Force plane out over the Gulf of Mexico to test its guns. Then there were navigation exercises over the open sea. Finally it turned inland on its main mission – to make mock attacks against ground radar stations to check the alertness and efficiency of their crews.

Many Americans had asked why, when the United States had such aircraft, they were not used to track the mysterious sightings which had so often been reported as flying saucers. America had the most advanced and the largest air force in the world.

Why couldn't the US Air Force track down the intruders?

The Air Force had tried. Again and again, fast interceptors had blasted up into the skies, only to find that the intruders mysteriously vanished at high speed, or that the UFOs were really IFOs – refractions of street-lights, or the tail of a comet, or the flashing navigation lights of an airliner.

But now a UFO had been sighted.

Not only sighted, but confirmed as an intruder on the sophisticated electro-magnetic scanners of the RB-47. Major Chase had been about to turn for his target when the

30

brilliant white light had moved away at a fantastic speed.

What kind of object could move at that speed?

Major Chase wanted to know. So did his crew. But they were uneasy. Other pilots had followed strange objects about the sky only to find that they had been heading for distant oil-well flares or the sun's reflection on an observation balloon.

Major Chase reported what he had seen.

'We had visual contact, and now we have radar signals from it.'

And then he asked for permission to pursue the intruder.

'Permission granted,' he was told. 'Get it!'

All jets in the area were diverted so that the RB-47 could track the intruder. His commander wanted to know what could fly at several times the speed of the new reconnaissance jet. Standing orders said that all reports of unidentified flying objects should be investigated. Too many of the high-speed intruders were around.

By 1957, the American government very much wanted to know what was behind the sightings. The RB-47 was the ideal plane to investigate. What made the pursuit more important was that the ground radar stations had made contact with signals from the mysterious object.

The chase lasted for an hour and a half. It covered hundreds of miles, with the scanners aboard the RB-47 in contact with the intruder for much of that time. Electronic direction finders pin-pointed signals as it flashed across the south-western states of America.

Twice the fliers aboard the RB-47 sighted the UFO. Major Chase had to swing the big Air Force jet sharply away at one point, to avoid being on a collision course with the mysterious bluish-white intruder. Their final sighting came as the fuel tanks were emptying fast. The UFO was beneath them; Major Chase turned the jet downwards.

From a height of six miles, the Air Force plane dived through two miles of clear sky to intercept the UFO. It was the last chance of making contact with the intruder.

The ground radar stations were still tracking the UFO.

But when the RB-47 was about to pass the UFO, it

suddenly vanished. At the same time – at exactly the same moment – it also disappeared from the scanners aboard the jet, and from the scopes of the ground radar stations.

A firm contact had gone in a moment.

This was not a case of a single flier observing a mysterious object which he alone saw. It was a UFO sighting, with back-up electro-magnetic readings.

But it was as frustrating as all previous UFO sightings – even with the latest electronic devices it was not possible to prove that the UFO was a machine from beyond Earth. It moved faster than the aircraft of the time. It accelerated at a huge rate. That was all that could be said about it.

An official inquiry some years later by the United States Air Force carefully considered the reports submitted by Major Chase and his crew. *Was he mistaken? Was he tracking an intruder?* Or was this another chase after something that was freakish but entirely natural, like the re-entry of a rocket or a huge meteorological balloon?

It was and still is an unidentified flying object, was the verdict of the scientists who advised the Air Force.

Since the 1950s, radar has become more powerful and more sophisticated, and many so far unexplained radar contacts can now be classified as IFOs. Under certain conditions, radio waves bounce about the atmosphere in odd ways, and they have confused radar operators in the past. Flights of birds and swarms of insects have appeared on glowing radar screens and been taken to be UFOs.

But not now.

Would today's radar be able to clear up the mystery of the UFO which Major Chase saw, and which appeared on both ground and airborne detectors for so long?

'Maybe,' cautiously say the electronics experts.

But they admit that modern electronics equipment is highly sensitive. *How sensitive*? 'We can pick up a fly twenty kilometres away.'

This kind of pinpoint accuracy was reached, though, by the astronomical telescopes of a century or more ago. The giant and amazingly powerful telescopes such as that at Mount Palomar in the United States have opened up the night skies so that we can see distant galaxies thousands of light-years away. It was a routine matter for such telescopes to survey the planets long before the first lunar expedition. Even quite small telescopes can be used to make an accurate map of the Moon.

How was it then that astronomers rarely sighted a UFO during the years when UFO-spotting was taken up by so many people during the 1950s? If astronomers could find new galaxies and explain the structure of our own star-system, why couldn't they pick up something that was only a few miles away?

A look at a telescope gives the answer. Telescopes are long tubes. If you look up at the sky through any long tube, you'll only be able to see a small part of the sky. And if the telescope is focused on a distant object, anything nearby that it picks up will be at best a hazy blur.

An astronomer would have to be extraordinarily lucky to catch a UFO passing his tiny cone of the night sky; and anyway, he'd be looking for something millions, or perhaps millions of millions, of miles away. But what is useful for verifying night sightings of UFOs is the kind of optical instrument that measures the amount of light in the sky. It's a more accurate version of the ordinary light-meter which tells an amateur photographer how to adjust the aperture of his camera to get the best pictures. Through the night, sensitive light-detectors measure the brightness of the sky.

The Earth turns, and the major constellations appear over the horizon. As each star-system brightens the sky, the light-meters show the level of brightness, which is recorded on a graph. High readings are peaks – the great flaring mass of Orion, the Zodiacal Lights and the Andromeda Galaxy provide such readings.

Photometric print-outs are studied. Do they ever show unusual peaks? Do they detect any UFOs? 'No,' say astronomers. 'UBOs.'

Unidentified bright objects are regularly recorded by night-glow photometric recording instruments. Some turn out to be missiles from testing-ranges. *IBOs*. But there are

33

recordings which cannot be explained. They may show up as having a brightness that would make them small stars, if they were stars. They are not all stars.

However, that is all that can be detected by such devices – strange bright lights, which remain a mystery.

How else can you scientists help track the intruders? The Air Force of the United States repeatedly asked this question. Soon after the first reports of flying saucers, a project began to list and classify all sightings of unidentified flying objects. It was called Project Blue Book. By 1967, more than thirteen thousand reports were listed. Most had been analysed and classified as IFOs, though.

As more advanced techniques of tracking – both visual and by radio waves – were developed, it became easier and easier to identify mysterious objects in the skies.

The flight of UFOs that flashed across many states of America on the night of 3 March 1968 alarmed and amazed the hundreds of people who observed it; but the cause was soon established. Most reports described a craft that looked like a World War I Zeppelin.

'It was huge, with a cigar-shaped fuselage and a row of port-holes,' said one informant. 'The weirdest thing was that it was completely silent!'

'Yes, it was metal,' confirmed another witness. 'It let out a trail of orange-yellow sparks, and did it move fast!'

'I saw the saucer coming at me over the tree-tops. It was like a big jet but faster!'

'I saw the rivets in the flying saucer,' one man reported. 'It was as close as that!'

Sightings were reported over an area covering thousands of miles. When the reports were collected, it was clear that there had been more than one UFO over the United States.

'Is this a new invasion by the flying saucers?' asked some newspapers.

'No,' said the investigating team.

They checked the visual reports against radar trackings and saw that there was a pattern in the sightings. The hundreds of witnesses who saw the UFOs were not mistaken –

they had seen the night-sky lit up by intruders from beyond Earth.

Not far beyond Earth though.

The UFOs were metal. They had been put together with rivets. And there were configurations on their sides that might have easily been mistaken for port-holes. They were part of a Russian scientific satellite known as Zond IV. The UFOs were large fragments of the satellite plunging through Earth's atmosphere and burning up with the intense heat of re-entry. Something had gone wrong with the control systems of the satellite: *IFOs, not UFOs*.

A statement from Moscow confirmed what the scientific investigators found. 'It's ours,' said the Russians.

Father Gill's flying saucers came under the expert study of a scientist who specialized in analysing UFO sightings. The reports from Papua were taken very seriously by large numbers of people who wanted to believe in the possibility of Earth being visited by extra-terrestrials, but it had soon become obvious to astronomers that Father Gill had been looking in the direction of the planet Venus when he saw his flying saucers and their crews.

'OK, so Venus was in the night sky,' they said. 'What of it? Father Gill saw a space-ship and what's more the crew signalled to him. How do you account for that?'

Astronomers explained. The atmosphere can play tricks with the eyes. Stars can look wobbly, planets seem to twinkle, the Moon can have a strange halo, and meteorites can even look as though they're travelling *upward*! And Venus can appear to change colour.

It gets worse if your eyesight is distorted. When you squint at a bright light or stare at it for a while then a number of odd effects occur. Rays of light flash from the light-source. After-images remain on the retina once you close your eyes, and they can split up into all the constituent colours of light. And, when your eyes are still open, you can see dust motes passing through the light.

What has all this to do with Father Gill's flying saucers?

One American investigator, Professor Carl Sagan, thinks it could have a great deal to do with them. For a start, he says, the UFOs are described in the reports as changing colour from white to green to red. Given the right atmospheric conditions, Venus can look like that.

But how about the shape of the UFO?

Professor Sagan experimented by looking at Venus through a variety of lenses. He remembered squinting at the stars and planets when he was a boy, and how the shape was distorted. So, he tried to distort the shape of Venus.

It wasn't long before he found a combination of lenses that gave a saucer-like shape, much like the one Father Gill had seen. Maybe Father Gill had poor eyesight and didn't know it!

That left the waving figures. Could they be explained as defective vision?

Professor Sagan is an astronomer who has given a great deal of thought to the phenomenon of UFOs. He believes that he has come up with a possible explanation that could account for the supposed contact by extra-terrestrials.

It's this: suppose Father Gill was *squinting* at Venus. If so, it might be that some of his eyelashes would come into his vision. They wouldn't be sharp and clear, because he would be focusing on an object at a considerable distance, so he might get an impression of a flattened sphere with a number of blurred lines above and below it. The four figures and the four legs of the space-ship could be Father Gill's eyelashes.

And the movement that he saw? You can try what Professor Sagan suggests – watch the behaviour of the dust motes when you squint. They move.

Astronomers, meteorologists, physicists, aviation experts – all who have an interest in strange occurrences in the skies – have contributed to our understanding of some of the mysterious events that can cause excitement and alarm, and which are known as UFOs. It is the task of the scientist to *find out*.

If he comes across a report of a flying saucer, one of the first questions he asks himself is, 'What else could it be?' It's an advanced form of detective work.

Sometimes the scientist looks at a photograph and remembers seeing an object just like the one that is claimed to be a flying saucer. So he tries to re-create what *might* have happened.

Flying-saucer photographs have turned out to be *frisbees* – one astronomer recalled seeing his son throwing a plastic toy into the air. He took a photograph of it, compared it with the flying saucer in the photograph submitted for investigation. The flying objects matched.

One of the most interesting pieces of detective work in this field was carried out by Mr Charles Gibbs-Smith, whose interest in aviation history led him to make an experiment after he had seen what was thought to be a film of a flying saucer.

An airline passenger had taken the film through the aircraft window on a flight from London to Glasgow, in 1966.

It showed a metallic object. Its shape wasn't unlike some reports of flying saucers. And it moved too fast for a plane.

Mr Gibbs-Smith investigated. He was convinced that there was some perfectly ordinary explanation of the UFO if only he could make a full analysis of the circumstances of the sighting.

How could he do it?

By making the same flight, in the same plane, in the same seat, and taking another film with an identical camera at the same time and at the same angle as the film he had seen.

He did it. He showed that the thick plastic of the window out of which he was looking could flatten a section of the tailplane and make it look as if it were an object completely separated from the rest of the aircraft.

Mr Gibbs-Smith had made a film of a flying saucer-like object just like that in the original film. You can see the kind of effect he produced by looking through the thick glass at the bottom of a bottle. Distortion produced the flying saucer.

Flying-saucer photographs have been shown to be nothing more than faults on the emulsion of the film – tiny blobs of chemicals that show up as dark discs. Trained photographic experts can soon spot them. They have to be on the look-out for deliberate hoaxes, which are easy enough to manufacture.

George Adamski claimed to have taken a photograph of a Venusian scout-ship, and certainly it looked like some kind of craft. There was a saucer-shaped hull, a dome on the top, and diffused light coming from the base of the craft. It could have been an extra-terrestrial space-ship.

'If it isn't though, what might it be?' asked an expert photographer.

He thought about the many objects that lit up the night sky.

It certainly wasn't a star or a planet. The shape was too regular. And the outline of the domed top was too clear for the UFO to be a missile or an aircraft. No, the photograph had to have been taken at fairly short range, since it was a night view.

He happened to look up one night and then hurried for his camera. The resulting picture looked exactly like Mr Adamski's photograph of the 'space-ship'.

What was it? *A street light?*

In 1952, the year Mr Adamski published his first book about the extra-terrestrials he claims contacted him, the big scare about flying saucers was on.

1952 is known as the year of the 'Flap'.

'SAUCERS HAVE LANDED!' screamed the headlines.

'ALIENS INVADE US AIR SPACE!'

'WHAT IS THE AIR FORCE DOING ABOUT THE SAUCER MENACE?'

The Air Force had responded by setting up Project Blue Book. By 1967 it had decided not to record any more UFO sightings.

'ARE THE SAUCERS HOSTILE?' the newspapers had asked fifteen years earlier.

'Not those we've seen,' said the Air Force chiefs.

Chapter Four

Mysteries of Time

Throughout the 1950s and 1960s scientists were constantly being asked 'Have extra-terrestrials visited our planet?' and 'Are flying saucers real?'

They could only answer that if someone brought along a flying saucer, or even a part of one, they'd look at it, work out how it was propelled, and then they'd be able to decide if it was extra-terrestrial or not.

Many people thought they had found a flying saucer, or at least a part of one. They took along their finds for examination. These included fuel reserve tanks dropped from fighter planes; meteorites; charred masses of plastic and metals; fragments of satellites and rockets; marker buoys washed up on the shore; wreckage from crashed aircraft; meteorological equipment from balloons.

The misshapen bits of burnt metal and the fragments of blackened plastic were examined closely. They turned out to be just what they looked like – bits of ordinary terrestrial scrap.

No one could prove that flying saucers existed. It was deeply disappointing to the many thousands of people all over the world who were convinced that the Earth had been visited by aliens in flying saucers. They asked again and again if scientists could account for the reported sightings – and they were given the usual answers. 'Yes, a UFO was spotted, and we think it's almost certain it was a double image of a star'; or 'Sure, but we've identified it as a sub-orbital missile gone astray'; or 'No, that flying saucer was a comet. Sorry.'

It was always the same story – proof was missing.

One man who was especially interested in bizarre happenings was Charles Fort. He spent a lifetime collecting evidence of weird and unexplained events in the latter part of the nineteenth century and the early years of this century. He found that there were thousands of reports of this kind. Huge blocks of ice fell from the skies. Enormous lights were seen by seamen and passengers on ocean liners. Silver-suited figures were seen in Europe. The sky rained frogs, blood and great chunks of iron. And no one, said Charles Fort, was interested!

He came up with an alarming idea.

Could it be, he said, that all these strange happenings were *deliberate?*

Was it possible, he asked, that *extra-terrestrials* were throwing things down at us, and occasionally landing on Earth themselves?

Charles Fort was scornful of the scientists of his time who paid little or no attention to these weird reports. He was convinced that they were important. He filled several books with the amazing stories he collected and, gradually, his ideas began to be taken seriously. By the time of the flying-saucer stories of the 1940s and 1950s, there was already a good deal of interest in the possibility of extra-terrestrial invasion.

Mysterious happenings of the past were again examined, like the violent and devastating explosion in the early years of this century in the forests of Siberia.

At around seven o'clock one June morning in 1908, farmers and wood-cutters in the Tungus area of Siberia heard an enormous explosion. The unlucky ones had their houses shattered as a hurricane roared across the forests. Roofs flew away and windows were blown in. The shock waves of the blast were recorded all over the world. The gigantic fireball left the sky glowing for three days. Rivers became rushing walls of water, and for an area miles across the forest was levelled. Ten miles from the centre of the explosion trees were set on fire. The temperature of the fireball must have been several millions of degrees.

What caused the explosion?

'A meteorite,' said the scientists of the time. 'The earth

has been struck by one of those masses of rock and metal which abound in outer space.'

It wasn't. The frozen ground of the Siberian forest floor had not been broken by the impact of a falling body. And what kind of meteorite could leave the sky aglow for three nights?

Could it have been a comet?

'No,' the astronomers said. 'Somebody would have seen the long tail of such a large body days or even weeks before the Tungus explosion.'

Over the next forty or fifty years, many theories were put forward, but the mystery remained. Nothing like the Tungus explosion had been recorded before that June morning in 1908, and nothing like it happened again – until scientists examined the effects of the first atomic bombs, and later the hydrogen bomb.

The hydrogen bomb explosion at Bikini in 1958 left clouds of gases which lit up the night skies. Earth tremors raced around the planet. And the fireball reached a temperature of millions of degrees.

Didn't such effects sounds like the 1908 Tungus blast?

'If a nuclear device was exploded above the forest at around five miles, it could have released the kind of force which blasted the Tungus area in 1908,' explained physicists.

Scientists investigated the blast area year after year and confirmed that larches in the forest contained radioactive isotopes – and the growth rings show that they date back to 1908. Tests with models showed that the explosion occurred about five miles above the forest.

How could a nuclear explosion occur nearly forty years before the invention of the atomic bomb?

It wasn't possible.

But there was scientific evidence of nuclear radiation dating back to 1908!

Here was a fascinating mystery!

The mystery attracted the attention of the UFO-spotters when Russian scientists announced their findings. And the flying-saucer enthusiasts began to put forward their theories.

'A nuclear explosion five miles over Siberia?' they said. 'That's easily explained. In 1908, an extra-terrestrial scout-ship visited Earth. Maybe it got into difficulties, or maybe it was carrying out some kind of experiment. Either way, it was the alien ship that was responsible for the Tungus blast.'

It is a fascinating idea.

Although no remains of anything remotely connected with alien space-ships have been found, no one can be sure that the Tungus explosion *wasn't* caused by extra-terrestrials. Some scientists point out that if an alien civi-lization wished to investigate Earth to see if we were a civilized race, it would be useful to send out a probe, much as our space-probes scan the planets of the solar system.

It might be that a robot space-ship was sent to Earth with a whole range of instruments to detect the kind of beings *we* are. If it turned out that there was anything interesting to report, the space-probe could be programmed to send out a signal.

And what better signal than an enormous bomb-blast, that would sent light-waves and radio signals back to the home star-system?

Could the Tungus explosion be just such a signal?

This kind of question is extraordinarily interesting to the flying-saucer enthusiasts and the UFO-spotters. All kinds of unusual happenings and recorded oddities attract their at-tention, but few scientists took these mysteries of the past as evidence that flying saucers did exist.

And then, in a completely unexpected and a tremen-dously exciting way, there did seem to be some kind of evi-dence that the Earth had been visited by aliens.

It happened like this.

An American astronomer became interested in ancient records of mysterious sightings in the skies. He was par-ticularly interested in Old Testament reports, such as that by the prophet Ezekiel:

'. . . as I was among the captives by the river of Chebar,' Ezekiel says, 'the heavens were opened . . . And I looked, and, behold, a whirlwind came out of the north, a great

42

cloud, and a fire infolding itself, and a brightness was about it, and out of the midst thereof as the colour of amber, out of the midst of the fire.'

What was so interesting about this passage?

Maybe, said the American astronomer, Donald H. Menzel, this was a flying saucer.

This was 1953. So far, the majority of scientists had declared that there was no proof of the existence of flying saucers. But here was an eminent astronomer and astrophysicist saying that maybe flying saucers had been spotted thousands of years ago!

Not only that, but in the Bible!

The idea appealed tremendously to UFO-spotters and those who believed in flying saucers. It brought together the very old and the very new – ancient documents and modern science.

The biblical passages were examined closely. What could Ezekiel have seen? He spoke of the heavens opening, a whirlwind, and clouds of smoke and fire – but out of the fire was more fire, the colour of amber. Didn't this description match up with the colossal burners of the first space-rockets? asked the investigators.

They looked at more of Ezekiel's vision.

Ezekiel went on to talk about strange beings with metallic feet which 'ran and returned as the appearance of a flash of lightning'.

Not only did these visionary beings move at the speed of light, they came, said Ezekiel, with wheels in the sky:

'And when the living creatures went, the wheels went by them; and when the living creatures were lifted up from the earth, the wheels were lifted up.'

It is a strange story, told in an archaic form. Ezekiel's language is full of vivid expressions that sound strange to us. But the UFO-spotters and the flying-saucer enthusiasts had no difficulty in working out what Ezekiel meant.

'It's obvious,' they said. 'All right, it sounds confused at first reading, but consider what he says again and again – there was something in the sky. And it produced an immense amount of light and heat. Then there were certain creatures that came with the light and heat. And how did these visitors leave? They were lifted up by wheeled vehicles, whose wheels folded up as they went. What does all this sound like?'

To them, it added up to a powered machine landing and then taking off again. What kind of machine?

Something like a helicopter: *a landing-craft from a spaceship!*

Our planet had been visited by extra-terrestrials in the ancient past, if this is the right interpretation of Ezekiel's vision.

Astronauts in the Bible?

Could it be true?

Professor Menzel began a new line of speculation into the question of extra-terrestrial visits when he first spoke of Ezekiel's vision. He himself said he was astonished at the interest his comments aroused.

In the 1960s and 1970s, scores of books and dozens of television programmes reported on the supposed remains of contacts with extra-terrestrials. Charles Fort led the way, with his books of weird happenings and his suggestion that extra-terrestrials could be throwing things at us. Once the idea got around, gradually the public became interested and wanted to know more. *Just who were these aliens?*

There was no shortage of inventive writers to tell them, as we shall see in the next chapter.

But meanwhile how does Professor Menzel himself explain the biblical flying saucers?

The starting-point for scientists when they consider reports of UFOs is generally something like this:

If it's not a flying saucer, what could it be?

Many of the usual answers can be forgotten: the landing lights of jet-liners, street-lights and hub-caps, meteorological balloons and parachutes, fireworks and flares, vapour trails and the flashing of warning lights from navigational buoys; all of these had not yet been invented in Ezekiel's time.

So Professor Menzel looked closely at what Ezekiel had written. *What exactly did he say he had seen?*

44

Wheels, said Ezekiel, *four wheels:* 'The appearance of the wheels and their work was like unto the colour of a beryl; and they four had one likeness: and their appearance and their work was as it were a wheel in the middle of a wheel.'

'The wheels of a helicopter-like vehicle sent down from a space-ship,' declared some researchers. 'This is a record of an alien visit to Earth.'

Professor Menzel stuck to the idea of Ezekiel's wheels.

What *could* they be if they weren't from a flying saucer?

For one thing, Ezekiel went on to say that the wheels didn't turn: '. . . they turned not when they went', says the Old Testament prophet.

Wheels that didn't turn.

Wheels that were the colour of beryl – a bluish-green colour, and that were amber too.

What could cause that kind of effect?

The astronomer thought about the effect of a dying sun through high cloud. In certain conditions, it can seem as though there *are* bright discs in the sky alongside the sun, and that there are spokes in turning chariot wheels.

The effect is an optical illusion.

Astronomers and meteorologists call the fake suns 'parhelia' or 'sundogs'.

Ezekiel's UFOs turned out to be IBOs. They are very rare events, but they have been seen by other observers.

Chapter Five

Stone Age Astronauts?

Clever researchers at once set out to investigate Professor Menzel's notion. Ignoring his own opinions, they dug out ancient maps, books and drawings to see if they could find more clues to the mystery of the ancient astronauts. They swarmed around the universities to ask famous archaeologists and historians if *they* had any ideas that might help them. Had they?

They had.

A number of scholars had speculated about the beginnings of civilization. Around ten thousand years ago, men in the Near East had begun to use metals, keep records and build cities.

Wasn't it all rather sudden? How did Stone Age man become civilized? Could it be, asked some scholars, that he had some help? 'Of course!' declared a number of inventive writers. 'It's clear that Earth was visited by astronauts in the distant past. Professor Menzel has explained that we should look in our earliest records for evidence of extra-terrestrials. So we'll look for Stone Age space-ships and space-men. Maybe primitive man himself recorded the landings of the aliens.'

It was an exciting time for the UFO-spotters and the flying-saucer enthusiasts. *Was* there any proof of astronauts visiting the Earth ten thousand years ago? The researchers studied reports and photographs from all over the world. They were looking for clues to the most fascinating mystery of modern times.

Stone Age astronauts!

Could it be true?

'Certainly,' the researchers said, after a while. 'There is clear proof that the Earth was visited by aliens of a superior race when the human race lived in savagery.'

Flying saucers in the Bible sounded strange enough to many people, but the thought of primitive man watching the landing of extra-terrestrials seemed absurd. Where was the proof of the alien landings? 'In cave-drawings and carvings,' explain the researchers. 'Stone Age man left a pictorial record of the astronauts in caves in various parts of the world.'

It seemed unbelievable.

Most people knew that wonderful paintings and drawings have been found dating back to Stone Age times. The caves at Lascaux in France are the most famous – prints of the galloping ponies, the charging bulls, the stags and long-maned horses, can be found in many homes. But where were the astronauts?

On the walls of a cave in Northern Italy, according to some writers. The pictures have been photographed. They show two figures, each wearing a suit and each with a tri-angular device in its hand. The figures look as though they are moving – the Stone Age artist has so arranged their limbs that they could be running.

But here is the thing that makes the figures different from most other cave-drawings: on the head of each of them is a domed head-piece, with spiky protuberances at the sides.

What do the figures represent?

'Astronauts,' claimed some writers. 'This is exactly how you'd expect primitive man to draw the aliens. The artist has got it all right – there's the dome, with the various bits of electronic and breathing gadgetry on the side. The space-suits are easily recognizable. And they're carrying some kind of measuring device, maybe to check on the Earth's atmosphere or measure radiation levels.'

It depends on your interpretation of the drawings, of course. Anthropologists say this: 'They're typical represen-tations of Neolithic Man.'

But how about the suits?

'It was cold in Stone Age Europe.'

And the domes?

'Masks. Primitive man thought wearing a mask would help the hunt along. It could be he's out to hunt stag.'

47

And the triangular devices?

'Stretch a bow and see what shape you get.'

Triangular.

Astronauts or hunters?

It's difficult to tell what the ancient artists were portraying. They are crude outlined sketches, like a young child's.

One drawing from the Sahara, said to be a Martian, shows a domed figure in a one-piece suit. The primitive artist who did the drawing had something strange in his mind when he was working – *had* he observed the landing of an alien? Certainly, the drawing is much like a young child's representation of one of today's space-suited astronauts.

Another picture, this time from Australia, not only shows a strange, human-like figure descending from the skies, but also a disc-shaped object above him.

'What more proof could you wish for?' say the flying-saucer enthusiasts. 'There's the astronaut and the flying saucer that brought him.'

So, according to a number of writers, such as Alan and Sally Landsburg, Robert Charroux, Louis Pauwels, Jaques Bergier and Erich von Däniken, who published books about their researches, Stone Age man *did* see the arrival of extra-terrestrials. He left drawings to record what he had seen. And, what was more, there were ancient myths that seemed to confirm that astronauts had visited our planet.

Myths are stories that are so old no one knows the truth of them. They are handed down from generation to generation for thousands of years, until their tales of gods and wars and magical happenings become part of every young child's education.

In Peru, the children of the Incas learned the story of Viracocha, the god of the people who lived in Peru before the Incas. The story is that Viracocha had come from some mysterious place over the sea to show the people how they might stop living like savages. He taught them to build cities and roads, how to weave and grow crops, and how to use metals. Viracocha left, but he promised to return.

The Incas decided that Viracocha should be their god too.

Unidentified flying objects over Salem, Massachusetts. A photograph taken by an American Coastguard in 1952. (Keystone)

Identified flying objects over Brazil. They look like Flying Saucers, but they're actually clouds. (Popperfoto)

How to take your own
Flying Saucer pictures.
An enamel plate, a
good camera and quick
reactions. (Rex
Features)

Below A Flying Saucer Identification lesson. This group of enthusiasts is based on Hampstead Heath. Note their chart of saucer types. (Keystone)

Nineteen-foot high cave drawing from Yabbaren, Tassili (Algeria) compared with line drawing of contemporary astronaut.

(Phayen Rich, member of ISTRA)

The Palenque 'Astronaut' from the tomb of the Mayan King Pacal.

(Phayen Rich, member of ISTRA)

Detail from a rock drawing in Val Camonica (Italy) – showing a primitive hunter, or astronaut? (Phayen Rich, member of ISTRA)

Rock painting from the Central Kimberley District of Australia, representing Vondsina, the personification of the Milky Way. (Phayen Rich, member of ISTRA)

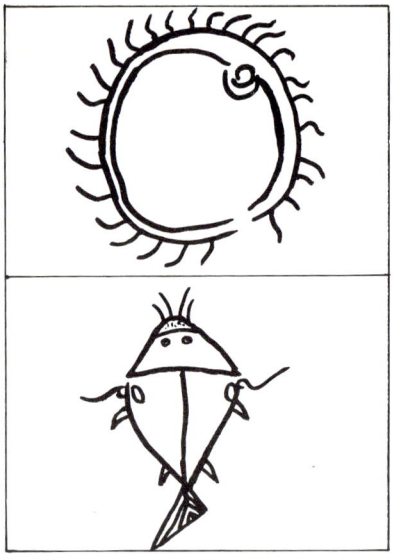

Dogon drawing of the 'Whirling descent of the spaceship Nommo' (*top*) and Nommo itself (*bottom*).
(Phayen Rich, member of ISTRA)

Monkey figure from the Nazca Valley, Peru.
(Robert Estall)

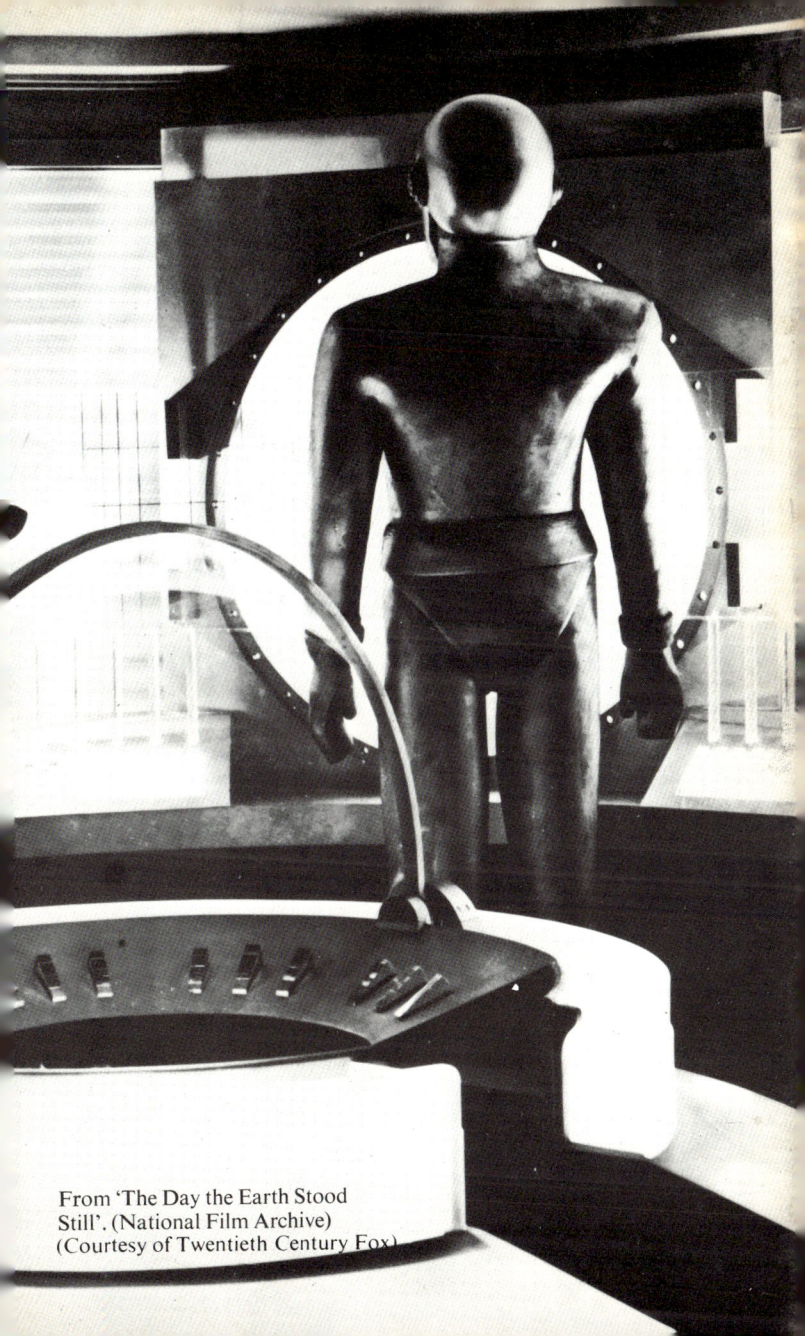

From 'The Day the Earth Stood
Still'. (National Film Archive)
(Courtesy of Twentieth Century Fox)

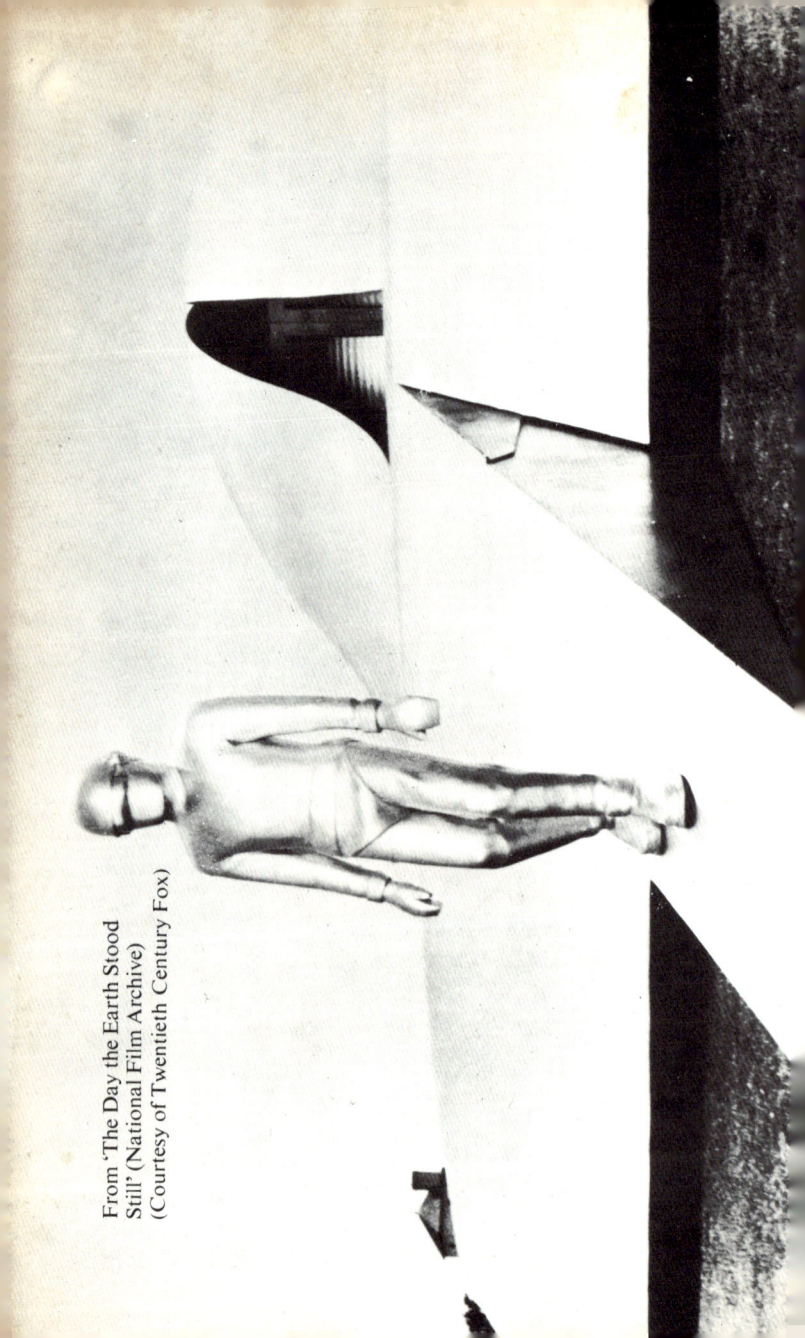

From 'The Day the Earth Stood Still' (National Film Archive) (Courtesy of Twentieth Century Fox)

When the Spaniards invaded Peru they found that they were welcomed. 'Viracocha!' the people called to Pizarro, the leader of the Spanish soldiers who had come to destroy them. 'Viracocha has returned!'

What has Pizarro got to do with Viracocha?

The ancient story goes like this: Viracocha was a huge white man with a beard. And he came to the land of the Incas from the sea.

Now he was back.

It made the task of conquering Peru easy, and the civilization of the Incas was destroyed by the Spanish visitors – the *Conquistadors*. Such was the Incas' belief in their myth that they allowed Pizarro and his men to march through their country and take their capital. They believed that the invader was their god He was tall, he was white, and he was bearded.

They had never seen anyone like that. It must be Viracocha!

But what has Viracocha to do with ancient astronauts?

'There has to be a connection between the myth of Viracocha of the Incas, and Quetzalcoatl of the Aztecs, and Kukulcan of the Mayas,' explain some researchers. 'They are all gods of the South American civilizations. And they were all said to be white and bearded.'

What have these three gods to do with astronauts, though?

'They *were* extra-terrestrials. They appeared, worked among the primitive people for a while, taught them the arts of civilization, and went away. Now, the astronauts are revered as gods.'

As proof of what they claim to have happened, the researchers point to the shape of some of the sculptures left by the people who built the mighty city of Tiauanaco. Amongst the stone carvings is one that has a helmet not unlike those worn by today's astronauts.

Another thing that stands out as strange, they say, is the way in which the massive stonework was constructed. Could these unknown people have managed to get blocks weighing hundreds of tons into position with only primitive

49

equipment? Or did they have help from bearded white strangers from the stars?

'Astronauts helped,' according to the writers who investigated this theory. 'And, what's more, they left guide-lines for more expeditions to Earth in the Peruvian desert near the ancient town of Nazca.'

The theory that was put together fascinated millions of readers. It mixed in the myths of ancient civilizations and the new stories of extra-terrestrials from flying saucers.

The ruins of colossal cities had been found in the jungles of Guatemala, in the towering mountains of the Andes, and in the deserts of Mexico. And, added to that, was the discovery of mysterious markings in the desert which covered miles, without any apparent reason.

The markings are known as the Nazca lines. They are grooves in the sand around four inches wide which score the desert in geometrical shapes. There are triangles and other regular figures. Some lines run together like a railway track. Others intersect at what seem like random angles, whilst other lines make up enormous pictures of birds and animals.

And they have been there for nearly three thousand years. *What were they for?*

'Quite possibly,' say serious researchers, 'they were used for astronomical observations. They could tell the positions of the Sun, the Moon and some stars and planets. Ancient peoples needed an accurate calendar. That's why they built megalithic structures like Stonehenge, for instance.'

And how about their connection with supposed astronauts?

Some of those who write about flying saucers declare that the Nazca lines are a message to visiting extra-terrestrials. They could, it is claimed, mark out landing strips for spaceships. Landing strips for space-ships? Statues of astronauts in deserted cities? Mighty buildings erected with alien help? *Could it all be true?* As with the cave-drawings left by the Stone Age artists, it depends on your interpretation of what you see.

Architects who have examined the cities of the early South Americans say that such structures could have been put up with levers, ropes and pulleys. The pyramids of Egypt are known to have been built in this way – tomb-drawings show how the Pharaohs' workers handled the enormous stones, with log rollers and ropes.

Muscle and intelligent planning could have built the cities of the ancient South Americans.

How about the statues of space-men? It could be, argue the writers who put the case for ancient astronauts, that many landings were made in the past. Old Japanese carvings, jade statues from Peru, and stone monoliths from all over Central and South America, are said to be representations of astronauts. Many have a resemblance to space-helmeted astronauts.

But, answer anthropologists, it's usual for representations of gods to be helmeted. Most gods were kings and warriors – and they'd need a helmet in their battles. The fact that they wear unusual head-gear doesn't make them astronauts.

As for the lines on the desert at Nazca, mathematicians have studied them and agreed that they were probably used as calendars. They are examples of early astronomical records. They could be useful to determine when to plant crops, when to expect rain, and when the frosts would come. But it's unlikely that they were landing-strips for space-ships.

'Would a space-ship need guide-lines that were five miles long?' asks one critic, Ronald Story. 'Anyway, aren't flying saucers supposed to take off vertically?'

The amazing carvings in the Peruvian desert *had* a use. Maybe some of the symbols, like the enormous humming-bird, did mark an unusual event in the history of the people who made them. We don't know.

Many people *want* to believe in Stone Age astronauts. They *want* to be reassured that other worlds than ours contain intelligent life, but unfortunately for them, what seem at first to be mysteries of the past turn out to be unusual but explainable.

Professor Menzel showed that the vision of Ezekiel's four-wheeled space-vehicle could have been what astronomers call a 'sundog'. The same kind of scientific investigation showed that what seemed to be a representation of

51

an ancient astronaut was certainly something odd, but not alien.

It is a Mayan carving from the lid of a tomb.

The Mayans lived in what is now Mexico. They built huge cities and, like the Egyptian Pharaohs, their kings raised enormous pyramids as their tombs. On the lid of the stone coffin of one of their rulers, who was buried at Palenque, is a complicated carving. It shows a human figure that seems to be reaching out to the strange objects above him as if he were making adjustments to them.

All around the figure are more carvings of such complexity that they totally confused the early writers who examined them.

'This,' they said, 'is an astronaut at the controls of his space-ship. You can work out the shape of the ship – there's the pointed top. At the base are the exhaust flames and gases.'

Scholars investigated. 'It's no astronaut,' they decided. 'It's a king called Pacal. He died in AD 683.'

Then how about the shape of the rocket and the exhaust flames and gases?

'The Mayans made patterns of animals, beasts and monsters and the corn-plant. If you examine the various parts of the carving, you'll find all of these in it. There's a quetzal at the top, and the roots of a corn-plant at the bottom. Your astronaut is sitting on a mythological creature, some kind of earth-monster. His hands are together because he's praying.'

The Palenque 'astronaut' was not piloting a UFO. He was a king passing from life to death. The carving shows him falling into an after-life, not piloting a space-ship.

This was another ancient mystery which careful research had solved. If Charles Fort had still been living, he could not have complained about today's scientists. They are on the alert to investigate any report of UFOs, flying saucers and extra-terrestrial visits in historical records.

However, it seems that as fast as new theories about extra-terrestrial contact are put forward, one by one they are shown to be something fairly ordinary.

Are there *any* ancient records that remain a mystery?

Robert K. G. Temple believes so. He is convinced that our planet was invaded by aliens from Sirius. They came here, so he says in his book *The Sirius Mystery*, at least six thousand years ago, and brought civilization.

Sirius is the brightest star in the sky. It was known to the Egyptians, who called it the 'Dog-Star'. In the last century, it was noticed that Sirius seemed to wobble. Something was causing it to move in an odd orbit. It had to be a heavy mass to cause this kind of wobble.

Astronomers proved that a dense 'white dwarf' star was responsible. With a powerful telescope, Sirius' attendant star can just be seen. Without one, of course, it is invisible.

How was it then, that Sirius B, as it's called, was known to the wise men of a primitive tribe in Africa? Anthropologists investigating the tribes who live at the edges of the Sahara desert were astonished by the astronomical knowledge of the Dogon people. When they were asked to make drawings of the star-system of Sirius, they showed the positions of the Dog-Star and also the tiny white dwarf, Sirius B. It was unbelievable.

They knew that the Earth rotated on its axis. They knew that Jupiter was circled by a number of moons, and that Saturn was ringed. They knew that our Sun was part of a spiralling star-system and, of course, they were right. Their knowledge has been handed down for thousands of years, from one generation to another.

Where did that knowledge come from?

Mr Temple links the Dogon people with the civilizations of Egypt and Sumer. It could be, he states, that the primitive tribe which now lives in Mali is descended from Greek settlers who took with them legends and myths of the Egyptians. In turn, the Egyptians gained *their* knowledge, as did the ancient Sumerians, from aliens – Sirians! Otherwise, runs Mr Temple's argument, how could the Dogon know about a tiny star they wouldn't be able to see?

Mr Temple says he doesn't believe in flying saucers. He does think, though, that one day the Sirians will be back to check on our progress. If they do come, we shall be just as shocked by their appearance as they were by ours. For another part of the theory that Mr Temple puts forward is that our extra-terrestrial visitors were amphibian.

Again, there are links with ancient drawings and written records. In Egypt, and in the ruins of tombs and temples in what were the civilizations of Babylon and Assyria, there are many pictures and carvings of gods and goddesses that are part-animal and part-human.

Some of them are fish-tailed. 'Proof of the amphibious nature of the extra-terrestrials from Sirius,' explains Mr Temple.

And the Babylonians spoke of the descent of beings from the skies. Their mythological creature Oannes has the tail of a fish, and he is said to be the founder of their civilization.

The Dogon people speak of such visits too. According to their legends, a great ark came spinning down to Earth. Mr Temple has located the area where they say it landed – to the north-east. And north-east of their original home is Eygpt. So, if the theory is right, the Dogon have preserved a memory of the visit of an interstellar ship.

From the ark, say the Dogon, came the Sirians. Their drawings of the invaders show a fish-like figure with a blow-hole for breathing. Mr Temple compares these figures with those from ancient civilizations, and with reports from Greek writers. Again and again, there are references to amphibious creatures who were intelligent, and who brought civilization.

Are the Dogon really in possession of information about the remote past when extra-terrestrials landed? Will the Sirians call in again, as the Dogon expect? It makes fascinating speculation.

Some scientists turn sour at any idea of extra-terrestrials visiting us, however. Why should they bother? they ask. The argument runs like this:

If aliens can reach us, by doing so they prove they're well in advance of our civilization. It also proves that we're inferior to them. So what could they want from us?

Anyway, if the ancient records really *do* prove that we've been visited by intelligent beings from outer space, maybe it also proves that they don't want to come back again. Maybe they've seen enough!

The many books written about ancient astronauts seem a long way from the first reports of Mr Arnold's silvery, shining discs – the flying saucers he spotted in formation over Mount Rainier. From questions like 'What are they?' and 'Why are they here?' interest turned to 'Have they been here before?' and 'Did anyone see them in past times?'

There *is* a connection between the flying-saucer stories and our interest in the origins of civilization. It's this: we're endlessly interested in the unusual, the extraordinary, the weird, the magical, in the things we can't explain. So we look for explanations; and we will continue to look for them.

Chapter Six

Other Worlds?

'The Martians have landed!' blared the radios in 1938, and thousands of Americans panicked. But it was Orson Welles' vivid radio version of H. G. Wells' novel *The War of the Worlds* that sent them streaming from the cities in fear of an alien invasion from the red planet. The frightened radio audience believed that they were listening to real radio news, when it was only fiction.

But it couldn't happen now.

When the Viking space-probe's lander settled on Mars, it began looking for signs of life. It took samples of the sand and rock and the atmosphere, and then robot instruments analysed and measured the results. There was no form of life. Mars has no inhabitants – it is an empty planet. There are no Martians.

Over the past twenty or thirty years, space-probes have sent back information about the planets of the solar system. They all report the same thing, to the disappointment of the flying-saucer enthusiasts: there is no advanced life-form on any of the planets.

The Moon landings proved that our satellite planet is dead. It is covered in gritty ash. The outer planets are too cold to support life, and if there is any life-form in the swirling gas clouds of Venus, Jupiter and Saturn, it's probably some form of micro-organism.

Experimenters made up laboratory samples of the atmospheres of the gas-covered planets to test the theory that they could support life. They found that some forms of life could live even at pressures a hundred times those on Earth, and at temperatures up to twice the heat of boiling water. But they are very elementary forms – probably much like the earliest micro-organisms on Earth thousands of millions of years ago.

There are no Martians, no Venusians and no Saturnians.

The people who claim to have been contacted by astronauts from these planets were mistaken. The more we learn about the solar system, the more certain we can be that there is no intelligent life apart from ourselves.

Astronomers and astro-physicists think, though, that other Earth-type worlds could exist. They point to the vast number of stars in our Galaxy. *200,000 million stars.* Out of this staggering number, astronomers calculate that a quarter, or even a half of them, will have a planetary system.

And many of these planets will be circling a sun like ours – a slowly cooling star which allows the gradual development of life on its attendant planets. Stars are found in pairs, and even in threes, so there will be planets warmed by more than one sun.

In our Galaxy, which is only one of millions in the universe, there could be thousands of millions of planets where life is possible. But on how many of these planets could there be intelligent beings able to reach out to other stars?

'None,' said scientists in past years.

Up to recent times it was believed that life on Earth began as a series of freakish accidents which couldn't happen anywhere else. But nowadays many scientists think differently.

Professor Carl Sagan, the American astro-physicist, thinks that there could be up to a million worlds in our Galaxy where civilized life-forms exist – good news for the flying-saucer enthusiasts. 'Obviously we have been inspected by beings who have perfected some form of interstellar travel,' they say. 'The parent ships remained in orbit around Earth and sent down smaller craft for surface landings.'

But Professor Sagan, as well as other modern scientists, points out a number of difficulties in the situation, one being that *too many* flying saucers have been seen.

The argument runs like this: There could be maybe a million civilizations capable of building star-ships. But on every world, that gives a million possible destinations for their ships. And if they were interested in visiting advanced civilizations, why should they seek us out? – after all, we can't reach them! We're probably low on the list of likely destinations – so how is it that there have been so many reports of flying saucers?

'It's more than likely,' say modern scientists, 'that we wouldn't be *noticed*. It's only in the last hundred years or so that we've used radio waves for communication, and our space-vehicles are so slow they'd take hundreds of years to reach the nearest stars. Anyway, we're on the edge of the Galaxy, where the stars aren't very close to one another. Interstellar travellers would investigate their nearer neighbours first.'

So the reports of flying saucers visiting our planet are suspect because there are so many of them. According to scientists like Professor Sagan, it's extremely unlikely that extra-terrestrials would find us interesting enough to visit, even supposing they noticed our existence!

But the idea of extra-terrestrial life has produced other theories. Scientists enjoy speculating about possible worlds. Another American, Harlow Shapley, has suggested that there may be intelligent life on planets that could be near us yet remain unseen. The reason we can't see them is that they have no suns.

Is it possible for planets to remain undetected?

It is, say astronomers.

In the immense gulfs between stars there are countless bits of rock, and there must be sunless planetary masses too. Enormous planets, perhaps a tenth the size of stars, and at least as big as the biggest planet in our solar system, could remain invisible to astronomers.

Mr Shapley thinks that a very large planet, which would be bigger than Jupiter, could have enough internal heat to support life without the need for sunlight. The enormous planet could be drifting in the gulfs of space between stars, gradually being pulled towards one or another of them.

Other astronomers calculate that there could be ten planets of such a kind between our sun and our nearest star-neighbour, Alpha Centauri. Could it be, they suggest, that our sun, over billions of years, has pulled towards it a sunless monster planet, on which there are intelligent beings?

'Quite possible,' say the large numbers of people all over the world who believe that George Adamski and a number of other Americans were contacted by extra-terrestrials. 'These theories prove that flying saucers do originate on planets near our solar system. There would be no problem in their crossing the distances involved. After all, David Swanner described a visit from beings from a planet on the other side of the sun – it can't be seen because it remains exactly opposite the sun.'

But there has been no proof of the existence of the kind of planet Mr Shapley spoke of. It's an interesting theory that happens to fit in with some of the flying-saucer stories of the 1950s and 1960s.

If we wish to be sure of the existence of extra-terrestrial life, we may have to develop space-vehicles capable of reaching the stars. The difficulty is, of course, the immense distances to be covered. We're used to the term *light-years*, but it's easy to forget what astronomers mean when they talk of a *light-year*. Light travels at 186,000 miles a *second*. It takes about eight minutes for the light from the Sun to reach us. If we could travel at the speed of light, a journey to the next star, Alpha Centauri, would take us over *four years*. And the rocket-launched space-vehicles of today would take many lifetimes to make the trip, even if they could carry enough fuel – which they can't. Enormously powerful though they are, the monster three-stage rockets seem feeble and slow when considered for use as interstellar space-ships.

In the early days of chemical rockets, scientists did look at the possibility of sending out space-vehicles using the thrust from rockets like those that put man on the Moon. If enough fuel could be carried, it was feasible to reach the stars. But it would take thousands of years for a round-trip.

No one lives that long, so one physiologist looked for an answer in the way that some animals live through the winter months in hibernation. Maybe space-travellers could do the same.

'Freeze them,' he said. 'When they get there, unfreeze them. That way, you expand their life-spans enormously.'

Only writers of science-fiction looked at the other

problems – what would happen when a crew returned, to find, perhaps, that they had been forgotten, or that time had played weird tricks on them?

Scientists nowadays have lost interest in chemical rock-etry as a form of interstellar travel. It's too slow. Some physicists considered the possibilities of harnessing the fast-est thing known – *light*. If only it was possible to build an engine that could generate what physicists call a photon thrust, then a space-vehicle could gradually work up to the speed of light itself – but no one knows how to begin to consider the engineering problems.

Engineers have suggested some remarkable schemes for powering star-ships though. A Canadian, Philip Norem, took up the idea of voyaging to Alpha Centauri by means of a space-ship which had huge reflecting surfaces. They would receive the thrust from a laser beam on Earth, and the space-ship would be pushed along as if it were a sailing-ship. When the astronauts reached their destination, they would have to build a laser unit to push them back to Earth.

Engineers looked at the power of the H-bomb too. Nu-clear fission, which occurs when a nuclear device explodes, releases vast quantities of energy. Could this energy be used to power a space-ship? One method looked at was the possi-bility of 'bombing' a space-vehicle to huge speeds by ex-ploding hydrogen bombs behind the ship. A less drastic kind of power-source would be to use nuclear fusion, of the kind that is the source of the Sun's energy – though attempts to make such a power-source are still at the experimental stage.

But even if such an engine could be built, using nuclear fusion as the Sun does, the problem is still how to carry the fuel. The distances are so great that no interstellar craft could possibly get to its destination without re-fuelling.

A rocket engineer called Robert Bussard came up with a simple answer: 'Re-fuel as you go along.' His idea was simple and remarkable. It was to build a huge scoop, shaped some-thing like the spoon of an ice-cream ladle, to collect hydro-gen from the clouds of interstellar gases and use it in a fusion reactor to power the space-ship. The scoop would have to be enormous – a hundred miles across – to collect the hydrogen needed, and Mr Bussard himself says that we have not yet got the capability for making a fusion engine for burning the hydrogen. But ideas like his show that serious thought is given now to interstellar travel. Scientists say that the only thing stopping us investigating beyond the solar system is our lack of a technology to develop the ideas we have.

None of these projects would look like a flying saucer, however. What we *might* build looks nothing like what *might* have visited us.

Most flying saucers fall into one of two main types. They are either cigar-shaped or disc-shaped. And they are much smaller than Mr Bussard's design for a colossal scoop-ship, or the interstellar galleon which Mr Norem thinks could sail to the stars pushed by the 'wind' of a laser beam's thrust. By comparison, flying saucers are neat, small and easily manoeuvrable. 'Of course,' say the people who claim to have been in contact with extra-terrestrials. 'They're far more efficient than anything we've begun to develop. Flying saucers from other worlds are powered by the mightiest force of all – gravity.'

Could space-vehicles be powered by the force of gravity?

H. G. Wells wrote a famous novel nearly fifty years before flying saucers were thought of. The title was *The First Men in the Moon*, and it told how a scientist invented a substance that would repel the gravitational pull of Earth. Screens coated with this substance would actually push against Earth – using the force exerted by gravity itself. Professor Cavor was the inventor. No chemical rocket was necessary to push Professor Cavor's moon-ship away from Earth. And it could reach staggeringly high speeds, as it used gravity to build up its velocity.

And how did the moon-ship slow down? The fictional astronauts reduced their speed by exposing the anti-gravity screens to the Moon's gravitational pull.

This was fiction, though, with no claim to reality. Yet the novelist H. G. Wells was himself a scientist, and at the time he was writing, many inventive thinkers were re-shaping ideas about space, time and the forces that move planets and

61

stars and star-systems. As long ago as 1901, he was using, in *The First Men in the Moon*, the latest ideas about the possibilities of interplanetary travel, just as nowadays engineers and technologists play around with the newest scientific ideas to see if some kind of engine *could* be built.

One engineer who asks us to look seriously at the possibility of gravity-powered UFOs is Leonard Cramp. Most scientists who have made a study of UFOs start with a fixed idea: if the sighting isn't that of a flying saucer, then what *could* it be? Mr Cramp doesn't work this way. Instead, he asks about the UFOs and the way they behaved in flight and then goes on to ask: could any kind of powered machine behave like that? What, asks Mr Cramp, are the flight characteristics of the UFO? And, in particular, what happens when a UFO takes off?

Most reports of flying saucers taking off from Earth describe how a disc-shaped machine rose vertically into the sky. Sometimes there are flashing lights from the base of the machine, sometimes flames and fire. But mostly the machines rise slowly, and then when they are at about tree-top height, they suddenly accelerate at a colossal rate.

What's more, Mr Cramp points out, they leave a circular trail or wake of exhaust behind them, and there is very often a kind of whooshing noise as they begin their climb.

What kind of power source could produce that kind of effect?

Mr Cramp has written a book about the problem. He has spent many years examining reports of UFOs, and he considers that it is possible that the future of interstellar flight lies in developing gravity-powered space-vehicles.

His argument runs like this: Gravity is the force that pulls us to a larger body – if we jump, the gravity of Earth pulls us back down. So, gravity is like a wind or a tide pulling us in one direction: towards the bigger mass – Earth. Suppose, though, we had some kind of machine that would take *in* the force of gravity and use it to push with, then our space-vehicle would first be weightless, and then it could move upwards. It would then be possible to take in *more* gravitational pull and use it again as a thrust – and the process could happen again and again. By the time the space-vehicle had taken in and pushed out the gravitational pull of Earth three times, it would begin to move upwards. And it would move *fast*!

Such a space-ship would move away from Earth very much as the flying saucers are said to have moved – at first slowly, and then with a tremendous surge of acceleration. As for the whooshing noise that accompanies many flying saucers' flight, and the bright lights that sometimes flare from their exhausts, it could be that they are side-effects from the gravitational engines. Light and noise would be produced, and this would cause observers to see flaring exhausts and to hear strange noises. As the interstellar space-ship moved away, the light would grow smaller – and it would look like some of the UFOs that have been reported.

'It seemed to hover for a moment or two, and then it shot upwards straight into the sky,' said a witness in 1954. 'The flying saucer remained stationary for about a minute, then it accelerated at a fantastic rate.' This was a report of a UFO in 1961.

Mr Cramp does not claim that flying saucers are powered by gravitational engines. He thinks though that extra-terrestrials *might* be showing us the transport of the future.

It could be that we are in the position of the inventor Leonardo da Vinci, who made sketches of flying machines hundreds of years ago. He knew that powered flight was possible; but the technology to build aircraft was not available. Scientists know that enormous forces are available to power space-vehicles. As yet, though, we can't control these forces.

So, how *can* we get in touch with other intelligent beings?

Since the beginning of the century, when radio communication began, there has been speculation about radio messages from other planets. Could some of the strange background noises be alien messages? asked the early pioneers of radio. Odd Morse code messages were received in 1924, and at once there was a great deal of interest in the possibility that they might have come from Mars. Mars was close to Earth at that time, so early radio pioneers kept a listening watch for more messages.

We know they were wasting their time, of course, and it has been shown that the strange signals almost certainly came from ordinary transmitters which were affected by freak atmospheric conditions. But the 'Martian messages' did create a good deal of interest in the idea of communicating by radio with extra-terrestrials.

By the 1960s, powerful radio telescopes had been developed which could scan interstellar space for transmissions by intelligent beings on other planets. Was it possible, asked scientists, that on planets circling the nearer stars, someone was sending out radio messages?

An American radio astronomer, Frank Drake, set up a listening and recording programme. He called the programme 'Project Ozma' – after the famous story about the Wizard of Oz. For three months Mr Drake listened for signals from two stars which were very much like our Sun, Tau Ceti and Epsilon Eridani. Were extra-terrestrials on their planets signalling to us?

Project Ozma was a disappointment. No signals were received.

Radio astronomers in many countries have set up search programmes for signs of extra-terrestrial life in the Universe, and there is a plan for making an enormous 'orchard' of radio telescopes which would pick up radio signals from 1,000 light-years away. The name given to this plan is 'Project Cyclops.' Like the one-eyed giant from the Greek legend, the radio telescopes would stare into interstellar space continuously, always alert for the faintest hint of a signal from the stars.

Some of the more recent scientific ideas about space-travel go far beyond just listening for messages, or building star-ships. They sound more like science-fiction than serious scientific research. Already scientists are discussing the possibility of transmitting human beings by light-waves. The tiny particles which make up the human body would be sent individually through space, and then reconstituted at a receiving centre.

There is talk, too, of *tachyons*. These are particles that *might* exist – if they do then they would have to travel faster than light. And if they do exist, argue scientists, then we could go on to consider how they might be used. So far, though, tachyons are just fanciful notions, but if they *are* in existence, and if they *could* be harnessed, the whole Universe could be opened up.

Flying-saucer enthusiasts were not surprised that scientists should take ideas like matter transmission and gravity waves seriously. 'Look what happens when flying saucers take off,' they say. 'There have been cases where a flying saucer has blotted out the electricity supply of whole districts on take-off. This happens because the gravitational field of the engines disturbs all power-sources.'

And there are reports of flying saucers hovering over cars, causing electrical failure. The car engine dies, and the lights go out. 'Powerful force-fields are responsible,' the flying-saucers believers say. 'You might call them gravity waves.'

And matter transmission?

'Look what happened to Allen Noonan,' the enthusiasts say. He was the American bill-poster who suddenly found himself transported across space to a mysterious hall. He claimed also to have visited Venus by some form of instantaneous projection. According to enthusiasts who believe that flying-saucer people from Venus have been in contact with us, the Venusians have developed ways of reaching across space that our scientists are only speculating about. 'They're far in advance of us,' claim the enthusiasts. 'What's more, if flying-saucer people hadn't visited Earth, there wouldn't be much interest in extra-terrestrial life.'

It could be so. Certainly, after the United States Air Force investigations into UFOs, a completely new form of scientist emerged. He is the exobiologist – the scientist who looks into the possibilities of life on other worlds.

Maybe there wouldn't be the branch of science called *exobiology* if there had been no flying saucers.

Chapter Seven

Flying Saucers at the Cinema

In the 1930s, science-fiction serials were very popular. *Flash Gordon's Trip to Mars* and *Flash Gordon Conquers the Universe* had accustomed audiences all over the world to space-ships, ray-guns, weird half-human creatures such as the clay-men, and power-crazy extra-terrestrials. Science-fiction films were in great demand, so when the flying-saucer scare began, it was natural that the film-makers should use flying saucers in their new productions.

Only three years after Mr Arnold told newsmen about the silvery, shining discs that looked like saucers flying, the most chilling of all the UFO films was made, entitled *The Thing*. It was adapted from a creepy short story by a well-known writer called John Campbell, Jr. The film, though, is more terrifying than the story. Film-makers in Hollywood knew how to keep audiences tense on the edges of their seats until the moment when the horrific alien comes to life – and this is what happens in *The Thing*.

When the film opens, a UFO is reported to have crashed near the North Pole. A tough Air Force investigator is sent out to check on the report. He is Ken Tobey, a man of action.

Locating the UFO is a simple matter. All that has to be done is to follow the tracks made by the intruder. And then the search party comes to the end of the tracks. The searchers look down. Tobey and his team realize that the glowing UFO came to a stop, melted the ice and sank. Then it was frozen over. They are standing above the UFO.

They spread out and stand at the edges of the strange, dimly seen craft. As they do so, the searchers realize that they are standing in a circle. What kind of craft could that be?

They have found a flying saucer!

Ken Tobey soon works out a way of reaching the ice-bound flying saucer – he uses a heat-bomb to melt the ice. But so great is the power of the thermite bomb that the alien vessel is completely destroyed. It is extremely frustrating for the scientists of the party. Just when the mystery of the UFO sightings might have been solved, an over-eager airman has to incinerate the evidence.

Only 'The Thing' is left.

It is an eight-foot alien, frozen in a block of ice.

Before a blizzard sweeps over the glowing remains of the flying saucer, the investigating team take the frozen body of the alien back to their base. The photography is superb, and the film begins to develop into a tense drama. What *is* the alien? And what will happen when the ice block surrounding him begins to melt?

It does begin to melt, of course.

An electric blanket is accidentally switched on in the freezing store-room where the alien is kept under guard. Slowly, the water begins to drip from the ice, and the guard doesn't notice. He is found next morning hanging in the store-room, the blood drained from his lifeless body! 'The Thing' from the flying saucer thrives on human plasma, and the base is under siege. From this point in the film the action is like many Hollywood suspense stories The thrills and chills come as the alien is tracked by Tobey. It turns out that a geiger counter can show the approach of the blood-crazy monster. The alien is radioactive.

'The Thing' is led into a trap. Tobey baits the trap with himself as the lure – and the geiger counter flashes and bleeps to warn of its coming. This is when the film makes its maximum impact. Will 'The Thing' enter the trap?

Fortunately for the members of the North Pole base it does, and 'The Thing' too is completely destroyed by fire. Nothing is left, neither of the alien itself nor its machine. The only advice that the film-makers offered to audiences was to keep alert – to keep watching the skies.

And that is just what the American Air Force was doing. When Howard Hawks made *The Thing* in 1951, large numbers of Americans believed that an extra-terrestrial invasion was certain.

Another film made in 1951 is usually recognized as the best of the UFO movies. It is *The Day the Earth Stood Still*, and is the story of an alien invasion by Klaatu, who arrives by flying saucer. His space-ship lands on the lawn of the White House, the home of the President of the United States.

A flying saucer parked on the Presidential lawn!

The Americans are amazed and frightened. Scores of Army vehicles roar through the capital, with grim-faced soldiers clutching automatic weapons. The streets are cleared, and citizens are warned to stay indoors. *The aliens are here!*

Soon, a ring of armoured vehicles surrounds the gleaming white space-ship, guns loaded and levelled. The excitement is tremendous, but the sight of the flying saucer lying without sound or movement gradually makes the watchers silent. The riddle of the flying saucer is about to be solved – cinema audiences held their breath. What would the aliens do?

There was only one extra-terrestrial visitor, however. An opening slowly appeared in the side of the huge white hull of the disc-shaped craft, and a tall man in a gleaming suit walked down a ramp towards the tense Americans. Klaatu was played by Michael Rennie, an actor with a lean and powerful face and deep-set eyes. He looked serious, and what he had to say *was* serious.

Klaatu brought a warning: *stop using atomic power*. He ordered the nations of Earth to stop developing atomic power, or the consequence would be the destruction of the world through devastating nuclear wars.

Here was the first contact with an extra-terrestrial civilization, and here was proof that aliens were ahead of us technologically. When the politicians delayed in answering, Klaatu showed how powerful the gleaming white space-ship was. He warned that he could do what the title of the film suggests – he could make the Earth stand still.

It wasn't the Earth that stood still, though, it was the

machines. Everything that used electricity stopped dead for thirty minutes as the extra-terrestrial vessel hummed into life and altered the force-fields of the whole planet. We see cars, trains, aircraft, factories, telephones and television equipment, all out of action. Klaatu had shown his strength.

But, argued the leaders of the nations of the world, he was one man, in one ship. There was only one flying saucer. However powerful it might be, couldn't it be handled by the might of the armed forces?

The politicians are still at their debates when Klaatu tries to return to his ship. Frightened soldiers open fire, killing him. The shooting of Klaatu begins the most thrilling sequences of the film.

What will happen now that Klaatu is dead?

We see Gort stir. Gort is the towering, massive robot programmed to aid his master. And Gort knows that his master has been killed. The watching soldiers see the flying saucer's side split and the ramp slide out. In the dark entrance a huge, squat figure can be seen. It is Gort.

Nothing can stop him. He brushes aside all opposition and finds the body of his master, which is then taken back to the flying saucer by the vengeful robot. For Gort is programmed to do two things now: place his master on a machine that will bring him back to life, and then turn the full powers of the ship on the planet that has harmed his master. The Earth will be destroyed.

The suspense is chilling. Seconds slide by, and we know that unless a woman reporter who has befriended Klaatu can reach Gort and say 'Klaatu Borada Nikto', then humanity is doomed. Fortunately, she succeeds in halting the destruct programme, and Klaatu recovers. The Earth has been reprieved – so long as Klaatu's instructions are obeyed. Otherwise, Gort would return!

The extra-terrestrial invader in *The Day the Earth Stood Still* turned out to be benevolent. Klaatu and his robot policeman were on a visit to explain the dangers we faced, not simply to attack us with the mindless rage of 'The Thing'.

Both these dramatic 1950's films added to the interest in

UFOs; and film studios followed up with more flying-saucer movies.

There were more hostile aliens in *Earth versus the Flying Saucers*, a film made in 1956, and in the Japanese film *The Mysterians*, produced in 1959. Both had marvellous scenes of flying saucers screaming through the skies which easily outmanoeuvred the rockets and jet-planes sent to engage them.

'The Mysterians' and the massive robots in *Earth versus the Flying Saucers* are out to conquer the world, as most cinematic aliens are, but again the hostile invaders are defeated. In both films, scientists find a means of destroying them.

In 1977, the aliens became friendly. It happened in *Close Encounters of the Third Kind*. We don't see them until the end of this long film, and when at last they appear from their miles-long space-ship, they're small humanoids about three feet tall, with strange wooden doll-like faces and limbs.

The plot of the 1977 film shows how attitudes towards UFOs have changed during the thirty years since Mr Arnold saw nine silvery flying saucers over Mount Rainier. Most early films about flying saucers showed horrific extra-terrestrials trying to conquer Earth, or grim-faced invaders warning us to stop meddling with nuclear power. *Close Encounters of the Third Kind* is very different.

It tells how two Americans, Roy Neary and Jillian Guiler, determine to climb the closely guarded mountain Devil's Tower. Roy Neary is convinced that this Space Agency Base holds the secret of the UFO he sighted, whilst Jillian Guiler is searching for her son, who was taken away in a flying saucer.

They are both right in thinking that Devil's Tower is the key to the mystery. American and European space experts have at last managed to contact the extra-terrestrials who have been watching Earth. Roy Neary and Jillian Guiler reach the top of the mountain as they arrive.

The scenic effects of the film are dazzling. The extra-terrestrials put on a fantastic display of lights to show that they are friendly, and then their enormous ship touches down on

Devil's Tower. It isn't a space-vehicle so much as a city – the exobiologists excitedly realize that the alien visitors *live* in the interstellar vessel. It is their home. They are wanderers amongst the stars.

Roy Neary and Jillian Guiler both find what they are seeking. Jillian's small son emerges from the alien ship, laughing and delighted to see his mother. *Where has he been?*

Like other humans, he had been taken aboard one of the smaller craft – the flying saucers – so that he could be examined. And now he was re-united with his mother, excitedly telling her how he spent his time on the alien vessel.

Roy Neary gets the biggest prize of all. He is to be one of a number of humans who will accompany the happy aliens when their interstellar ship resumes its million-year voyage.

It's easy to see why the film-makers liked experimenting with the flying-saucer phenomenon. They could build superb luminous space-ships, like the marvellous flying saucer in *The Day the Earth Stood Still*. They could show eerie aliens, spewing death-rays from their fingers, like 'The Mysterians'. And they could exercise their inventive minds in finding answers to the questions that began with the UFO craze of the late 1940s and early 1950s.

We're sure to see more UFO films!

Chapter Eight

UFOs Then and Now

What started the UFO stories?

Not Mr Arnold, according to researchers. Long before 1947 there were reports of strange flying machines.

Alexander Hamilton was asleep at his farm in Leroy, Kansas, when he heard his cattle moving around and making a noise. He got up to investigate.

'Pa, what's *that*!' yelled his son Walt.

Mr Hamilton was too amazed to speak. An airship three hundred feet long was slowly descending on to his pasture field!

The cattle milled about, one of them caught in a cable trailing from the airship. Mr Hamilton looked through the windows of the cabin. Inside were six strange-looking people. The airship had a large searchlight and also green and red smaller lights. Mr Hamilton and his son had seen nothing like it before. Very few people had seen any kind of powered aircraft, for this was April 1897. And not until 1900 did a motor-powered airship fly in the United States.

So what *was* the mysterious craft?

Mr Hamilton didn't know, but he could see that the airship was beginning to rise. And a heifer was entangled in its cable! The animal was also caught up in a fence. The Hamiltons managed to cut away the fence, but the cable still held the heifer fast.

And the airship sailed away with the terrified beast lowing and bawling as it rose into the air. Next day its remains were found miles away.

Airships were seen in many parts of the United States. They dropped in on farms and asked for water, collided with windmills, signalled to people below with streamers and lights, and sometimes explained who they were. Scores of airships were reported.

'We're from the North Pole,' explained one group of visitors. 'We're on a foraging trip – supplies are short where we come from.'

'They're from Mars,' explained journalists of the time.

'There are no airships,' scientists declared. 'The brightly shining objects described by witnesses are obviously stars or planets. Their apparent movement and change of colour is explained by the atmospheric conditions on the nights they appeared. Venus is a likely source of the mystery.'

Practical jokers confessed that they were responsible for some of the sightings, such as the balloon sent up over Burlington, Iowa in April 1897. Witnesses were sure that they had seen a genuine airship simply because so many airship stories were around.

But were there any airships? It's impossible to say, just as it's impossible to say that flying saucers made thousands of visits to Earth from 1947 onwards.

In 1897, there was a tremendous interest in the possibility of powered flight. For the past twenty years, experimenters had tried to construct airships, and soon they would succeed. Not only would airships be built; the Wright brothers would soon show the world that the age of the aeroplane had begun.

There was also talk of interplanetary travel. The astronomer Percy Lowell had just written a sensational book about 'canals' on Mars, which seemed to indicate that the planet was inhabited. H. G. Wells and Jules Verne had written stories about space-craft from Mars. So, when mysterious objects began to be reported in the skies over America in 1896, many people linked science-fiction and astronomical observation with the unidentified flying objects. It seemed obvious that if airships could cross the skies, there was no reason why they shouldn't travel between the planets. And if Mars was inhabited, maybe the Martians had come to have a look at us.

The idea of extra-terrestrial invasion by UFOs has been around for a long time.

So, when Mr Arnold's flying saucers were reported as travelling at speeds far beyond what seemed possible by our aircraft, there was a ready-made answer for the question 'What are they?' Half a century after the airships mystery, people reacted much as they had done in the 1890s: 'We're being invaded!' Maybe one reason for the immediate interest in the first flying-saucer stories can be seen in what happened (or didn't happen) fifty years ago.

There were other reasons, though. One was the 'Flying Flapjack', the XF-5-U-1. This was a circular-shaped aircraft the United States Navy had begun work on around 1940. Experimental work showed, though, that it was unmanageable, and the secret project was scrapped. Yet the name *Flying Flapjack* and the machine's unusual shape may have contributed to American Air Force interest in reports of flying saucers.

Circular aircraft had already been invented. During the war years there had also been reports of mysterious unidentified flying objects which were given the name 'Foo Fighters'. They appeared as balls of light and followed some Allied aircraft. Fighter pilots attempted to shoot them down, and radar operators tracked them. No one could explain what they were at the time, though it was believed that they could be some form of enemy weapon.

By the end of the Second World War, many pilots had discussed the strange sightings, and there had been investigations of the UFOs.

Flying Flapjack. Foo Fighters. Disc-shaped aircraft and glowing balls of light! Doesn't it sound familiar?

The Second World War saw the first big chemical rockets in action. When the war ended, German rocket engineers went either to the USSR or to America. It was the time of the Cold War, and the two powerful nations regarded themselves as potential enemies. It was a tense time. War could break out at any moment, and the new rocket technology was vital. The race was on to build the first intercontinental missiles.

Naturally, American military men were intensely curious about the USSR rocket programme; and naturally the

Russians developed their rocket-launchers in conditions of top security. What secret weapons were the Russians building?

And then, in June 1947, Kenneth Arnold saw nine disc-shaped UFOs moving at a tremendous speed quite near Washington!

'Martians,' said many people. They remembered *The War of the Worlds*. Some of them could remember the 'airships' of 1896–7.

'Atmospheric hallucination,' carefully explained scientists who had made a study of freakish weather conditions.

'*Russians!*' excitedly said some American military figures. 'The flying saucers are their new secret weapon!'

They remembered the mysterious Foo Fighters which couldn't be shot down. They knew that German rocket engineers were perfecting huge launchers. The wartime phantom Foo Fighters had manoeuvred at terrific speeds; and German V-2s could travel at thousands of miles an hour; and circular aircraft had been built!

To some military men, it all addded up. The USSR had developed aircraft which could leave any American plane standing.

There was an immediate inquiry. It soon reported that the mysterious objects might be UFOs, but they weren't Russian planes.

But rumours of the Air Force's fears fed public interest in flying-saucer stories. People who at first dismissed the stories as hoaxes or hallucinations began to take them seriously. Surely there was something to all the new reports of fantastic unidentified flying objects? Otherwise, why should the American Air Force take them so seriously?

In fact, by the early 1950s American Air Force investigators were fairly sure that nearly all of the sightings could be accounted for by natural causes. But there was so much secrecy about the findings of the investigating committees that many people were sure something was being hidden from them. There were press and television reports of a cover-up. *What was the Air Force keeping secret?*

There was nothing to be secretive about. Most of the

UFOs had turned out to be IFOs. And the few sightings that still hadn't been explained in the 1950s were almost certainly proved to be natural phenomena after intensive further investigation in the 1960s. But, because of the secrecy surrounding UFO investigation, there was even greater public interest! At the same time, the space-research programme focused attention on the possibilities of life on the other planets of the solar system. Added to this was the craze for books about Stone Age astronauts.

The flying-saucer phenomenon has lasted much longer than the first UFOs scare. After 1897, the airships mystery soon stopped interesting the public, but flying saucers are still exciting news. A whole new generation has grown up since the first silvery discs were spotted by Mr Arnold. Everybody knows about flying saucers, young and old. In one school in America, there was even a do-it-yourself construction kit for a flying saucer.

It happened in 1968, one early January evening. '30 CITIZENS SIGHT UFO', announced the *Denver Post*. The *Post*'s story went on to describe how witnesses saw a large round UFO flying over the town of Castle Rock, which is a small town near Denver, USA. The UFO seemed to one observer to be shooting out balls of flame as it passed over the town, whilst another witness said the only light from it looked about the colour of car headlights with mud on them. Twelve townspeople thought the UFO was large.

'Fifty feet long,' said Howard Ellis. 'And about six hundred feet above the town.'

But the Castle Rock UFO was soon identified.

A couple of days later, Mrs Dietrich of Castle Rock explained that her sons Tom and Jack had made the UFO in class at school. Their teacher had shown them how to make a balloon out of a clear plastic dry-cleaning bag – the kind that comes on a suit. The Dietrich boys may or may not have been trying to hoax the town, but certainly their homemade UFO caused a good deal of excitement for a couple of days.

There have been other hoaxes and deliberate attempts to delude the public. Always they caused great excitement.

76

Any news about flying saucers was interesting. In 1967, it seemed that a whole squadron of them had landed in England. They were found by road-sides in a line miles apart in the south, and at once they were identified; for what else could they be but flying saucers when they were domed, silvery discs which went 'Bleep-bleep-bleep!'?

A hoax. Technical students had succeeded in causing the flying-saucer scare. Inside the well-made discs were tape-recorders. 'Bleep-bleep-bleep,' they went, leaving the investigators baffled and the hoaxers delighted with themselves.

One man who deceived the public throughout the 1950s was George Van Tassel. He claimed to have ridden in flying saucers, and that a more advanced race had shown him how to build a machine which would make people young again. For years he lectured about his experiences, and it was not until 1959 that he was shown to be a liar.

What happened was that a lawyer sent him some photographs of flying saucers and their occupants. Mr Van Tassel declared at once that they were further proof of his claims. What he didn't know was that he himself was being deceived, and when he appeared on a television show he was dismayed to learn that the lawyer had set a trap for him.

The photographs were fakes. And Mr Van Tassel had said they were authentic! Yet even though George Van Tassel and others who claimed to have been in contact with extra-terrestrials were proved to be fakers and deceivers, UFOs continued to interest everyone. Even those who poured scorn on the whole idea of aliens landing on Earth were fascinated by the *idea* of flying saucers. It seems that there is something about UFOs that appeals to the modern imagination.

Why *are* they so fascinating?

Why have so many clubs, societies and organizations been founded to investigate UFOs?

Why is it that every new film about flying saucers attracts audiences all over the world?

And why is the idea of UFOs linked with ancient myths and legends and religions?

The UFO enthusiasm interested the famous psychologist

77

Carl Jung. He made a study of everything about flying saucers. What was it about them that so interested so many people? Was the answer to be found in the *mind* of modern man? Carl Jung thought so.

He read the accounts of contacts with extra-terrestrials and considered the reports of sightings. Everything he read seemed to him to be remarkable – and everything seemed to point to one conclusion. *UFOs are a modern myth.*

Myths are stories of mighty events in the dim past, when giants walked the Earth, when gods hurled thunderbolts from the skies, when great serpents circled the globe, and when dragons breathed fire at men. Magical, mysterious things were at work in the world.

In Indian mythology, there are stories of flying machines, and the Greeks tell how their gods could travel through space in an instant, changing their shape to suit their surroundings.

Myths and legends are the stories that in ancient times explained anything that men could not understand. If an earthquake devastated an area, then the gods were angry. If a wild storm wrecked a ship, then the gods had not received their due sacrifice. If there was an amazing sight in the skies, then some heavenly being was responsible. Gods roamed the skies!

It could be, explains Carl Jung, that we're seeing in the flying-saucer stories a new way of explaining those things we don't understand and which we fear. In the 1890s there was a scare over an airship invasion from Mars. Nowadays, we are divided between hopes of reaching the planets and the stars, and our fears of what we might find there! So, in our confusion, we seize on the stories of visits by vastly superior beings who might teach us how to live without wars and also how to build much better star-ships – when we deserve them.

How about the shape of the flying saucers?

Carl Jung points out that in ancient religion and mythology, the circle has a magical importance. For instance, saints are usually shown with a halo around their heads.

It's not surprising, then, that flying saucers – which are

mostly circular – have been connected with the ancient symbol for *gods* or celestial beings. The human mind wants to have things explained – and, according to Carl Jung, the way to understand why there is so much enthusiasm for UFOs is to look at the workings of the mind.

But do flying saucers really exist?

The famous psychologist thinks they do – *in the mind*. He points out that many accounts of contacts with aliens and quite a few of the flying-saucer sightings have a dreamlike quality. Maybe they are just that – vivid hallucinations.

UFO enthusiasts disagree. They point out that there have been more than 20,000 sightings of UFOs since 1947. Many of the witnesses have been trained observers, known in their professions as reliable men and women. Could all of them be mistaken or only half-awake? ask the enthusiasts. 'No,' they say firmly. 'Many sightings remain unexplained. It's up to organizations like ours to collect reports on sightings from all over the world. Patterns of sightings can be plotted and more learned about the reasons for the visits of flying saucers to our planet.'

All over the world, there are organizations for the study of UFOs.

In England there is the Interplanetary Space Travel Research Organization (ISTRA), which was founded in 1957; the British Unidentified Flying Object Research Association (BUFORA), set up in 1962; and the Unidentified Flying Object Research Society, which began in 1963.

There are scores of UFO research organizations in the USA. In 1952 the Aerial Phenomena Research Organization (APRO) was founded, and in 1956 the American government set up NICAP, the National Investigations Committee on Aerial Phenomena.

There are UFO societies in Japan, Finland, Germany, Canada, Argentina, Belgium, New Zealand, the Netherlands and Australia. They publish magazines such as *Ufo Skywatch*, *Ufo Log*, *Skylook*, *Ufo Nachtrichten*, *Orbit*, and *Flying Saucers Are Fact*, and they welcome new members.

Here is a questionnaire the UFO investigators use to record new sightings:

INTERPLANETARY TECHNICAL INFORMATION

This questionnaire has been prepared so that you can give the I.S.T.R.G. as much information as possible concerning the unidentified aerial phenomenon that you have observed. Please try to answer as many questions as you possibly can. The information that you give will be used for research purposes. Your name will not be used in connection with any statements, conclusions, or publications without your permission. We request this personal information so that if it is deemed necessary, we may contact you for further details.

1. When did you see the object?

_____ _____ _____
Day   Month   Year

(Circle One): a. Eastern
               b. Central
               c. Mountain
               d. Pacific
               e. Other _____

2. Time of day: _____ _____
                Hours   Minutes

(Circle One): A.M. or P.M.

(Circle One): a. Daylight Saving
               b. Standard

3. Time Zone:

4. Where were you when you saw the object?

Nearest Postal Address	City or Town	State or County

5. How long was object in sight? (Total Duration)

	Hours	Minutes	Seconds

    a. Certain   c. Not very sure
    b. Fairly certain d. Just a guess

5.1 How was time in sight determined?

Was object in sight continuously?   Yes _____ No _____

6. What was the condition of the sky?

    DAY   NIGHT
    a. Bright   a. Bright
    b. Cloudy   b. Cloudy

7. If you saw the object during DAYLIGHT, where was the SUN located as you looked at the object?

(Circle One):
a. In front of you
b. In back of you
c. To your right
d. To your left
e. Overhead
f. Don't remember

8. If you saw the object at NIGHT, what did you notice concerning the STARS and MOON?

8.1 STARS (Circle One):
a. None
b. A few
c. Many
d. Don't remember

8.2 MOON (Circle One):
a. Bright moonlight
b. Dull moonlight
c. No moonlight – pitch dark
d. Don't remember

9. What were the weather conditions at the time you saw the object?

CLOUDS (Circle One):
a. Clear sky
b. Hazy
c. Scattered clouds
d. Thick or heavy clouds

WEATHER (Circle One):
a. Dry
b. Fog, mist, or light rain
c. Moderate or heavy rain
d. Snow
e. Don't remember

82

10. The object appeared: (Circle One):

a. Solid
b. Transparent
c. Vapour
d. As a light
e. Don't remember

11. If it appeared as a light, was it brighter than the brightest stars? (Circle One):

a. Brighter
b. Dimmer
c. About the same
d. Don't know

11.1 Compare brightness to some common object:

12. The edges of the object were:

(Circle One):
a. Fuzzy or blurred
b. Like a bright star
c. Sharply outlined
d. Don't remember
e. Other _____

13. Did the object:

(Circle One for each question)

a.	Appear to stand still at any time?	Yes	No	Don't know
b.	Suddenly speed up and rush away at any time?	Yes	No	Don't know
c.	Break up into parts or explode?	Yes	No	Don't know
d.	Give off smoke?	Yes	No	Don't know
e.	Change brightness?	Yes	No	Don't know
f.	Change shape?	Yes	No	Don't know
g.	Flash or flicker?	Yes	No	Don't know
h.	Disappear and reappear?	Yes	No	Don't know

14. Did the object disappear while you were watching it? If so, how?

15. Did the object move behind something at any time, particularly a cloud?

(Circle One)   Yes   No   Don't know.   If you answered YES, then tell what it moved behind: _____

_____
_____

16. Did the object move in front of something at any time, particularly a cloud?

(Circle One)   Yes   No   Don't know.   If you answered YES, then

tell what in front of: _____

_____

_____

17. Tell in a few words the following things about the object:

a. Sound _____

b. Colour _____

18. We wish to know the angular size. Hold a match stick at arm's length in line with a known object and note how much of the object is covered by the head of the match. If you had performed this experiment at the time of the sighting, how much of the object would have been covered by the match head?

19. Draw a picture that will show the shape of the object or objects. Label and include in your sketch any details of the object that you saw such as wings, protrusions, etc., and especially exhaust trails or vapour trails. Place an arrow beside the drawing to show the direction the object was moving.

20. Do you think you can estimate the speed of the object?

(Circle One)   Yes   No

If you answered YES, then what speed would you estimate? _____

21. Do you think you can estimate how far away from you the object was?

(Circle One)   Yes   No

If you answered YES, then how far away would you say it was? _____

22. Where were you located when you saw the object? (Circle One):

a. Inside a building
b. In a car
c. Outdoors
d. In an aeroplane (type)
e. At sea
f. Other _____

23. Were you (Circle One):

a. In the business section of a city?
b. In the residential section of a city?
c. In open countryside?
d. Near an airfield?
e. Flying over a city?
f. Flying over open country?
g. Other _____

24. If you were MOVING IN a vehicle at the time, then complete the following questions:

24.1 What direction were you moving? (Circle One)

a. North   c. East   e. South   g. West
b. Northeast   d. Southeast   f. Southwest   h. Northwest

24.2 How fast were you moving? _____ miles per hour.

24.3 Did you stop at any time while you were looking at the object?

(Circle One)   Yes   No

25. Did you observe the object through any of the following?

a. Eyeglasses	Yes	No	e. Binoculars	Yes	No
b. Sun glasses	Yes	No	f. Telescope	Yes	No
c. Windscreen	Yes	No	g. Theodolite	Yes	No
d. Window glass	Yes	No	h. Other _____		

26. In order that you can give as clear a picture as possible of what you saw, describe in your own words a common object or objects which, when placed up in the sky, would give the same appearance as the object which you saw.

88

27. In the following sketch, imagine that you are at the point shown. Place an 'A' on the curved line to show how high the object was above the horizon (skyline) when you first saw it. Place a 'B' on the same curved line to show how high the object was above the horizon (skyline) when you last saw it. Place an 'A' on the compass when you first saw it. Place a 'B' on the compass when you last saw the object.

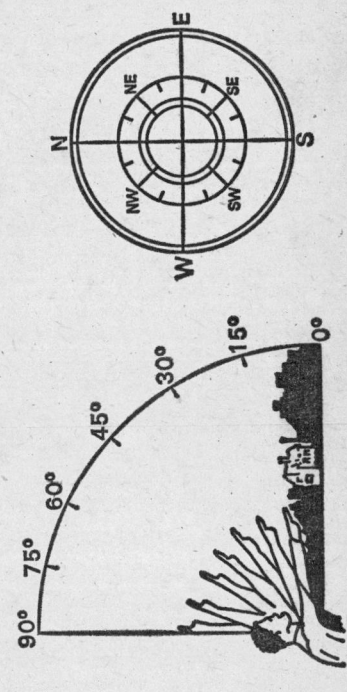

28. Draw a picture that will show the motion that the object or objects made. Place an 'A' at the beginning of the path, a 'B' at the end of the path, and show any changes in direction during the course.

29. If there was MORE THAN ONE object, then how many were there? _____
Draw a picture of how they were arranged, and put an arrow to show the direction that they were travelling.

30. Have you ever seen this, or a similar object before? If so give date or dates and location.

31. Was anyone else with you at the time you saw the object? (Circle One)   Yes   No

   31.1 If you answered YES, did they see the object too? (Circle One)   Yes   No

   31.2 Please list their names and addresses:

32. Please give the following information about yourself:

NAME _____ _____ _____
       Last Name   First Name   Middle Name

ADDRESS _____
           Street

TELEPHONE NUMBER _____ AGE _____ SEX _____

Indicate any additional information about yourself, including any special experience, which might be pertinent.

_____

_____

33. When and to whom did you report that you had seen the object?

_____ _____ _____
    Day   Month   Year

_____

92

The exobiologists and some astronomers agree that all sightings should be reported for further study. Allen Hynek, the American astronomer, is not a believer in flying saucers, but he does think that there is some new, unexplained mystery in the skies. Until we solve the riddle of the UFOs, he suggests that careful and accurate recording *may* possibly tell us something about them. He is not alone in giving this advice.

'Keep an open mind,' advise the scientists who have chosen to search for signs of extra-terrestrial intelligence. 'That's what science is.' They agree that though no one has proved that flying saucers have visited Earth, no one has proved they haven't.

Maybe that's the real reason for the fascination of flying saucers – a part of our minds says 'No, there can't be any such things!' whilst the hidden, secret part of us answers, 'Yes, but just suppose there were!'

It's the most exciting idea of our times.

Filmography

Chariot of the Gods
Film of the book by Erik von Däniken. Have extraterrestrials visited the Earth?

Close Encounters of the Third Kind
Directed by Steven Spielberg. Fictional work based on UFO cases.

Earth Versus the Flying Saucers
Special effects by Ray Harryhausen. Hostile aliens attack the Earth.

Escape to Witch Mountain and *Return from Witch Mountain*
Walt Disney comedies featuring visits to earth by flying saucers.

Starship Invasion
1977 film starring Christopher Lee.

War of the Worlds
Film of the book by H. G. Wells. Earth invaded by Martians.

Ufonauts
TV film containing interviews with people claiming to have met aliens.

Unidentified Flying Objects
A major film (from Universal) which takes a documentary look at UFOs.

Bibliography

George Adamski, *Inside the Flying Saucers*, Warner, 1967

Jacques Bergier, *Mysteries of the Earth*, Sidgwick and Jackson, 1974; Futura, 1975

Otto Binder, *What We Really Know about Flying Saucers*, Fawcett, 1967

Ralph and Judy Blum, *Beyond Earth*, Corgi, 1974

Robert Charroux, *The Mysterious Unknown*, Spearman, 1972; Corgi, 1973

L. G. Cramp, *Piece for a Jigsaw*, Somerton, 1966

Charles Fort, *The Complete Books*, Dover, 1975

Rupert Furneaux, *Ancient Mysteries*, Futura, 1976

Richard Harris Hall, *The UFO Evidence*, National Investigations Committee on Aerial Phenomena, 1964

I. Hobana and J. Weverbergh, *UFOs from behind the Iron Curtain*, Souvenir, 1974; Corgi, 1975

J. A. Hynek, *The UFO Experience*, Corgi, 1974

David M. Jacobs, *The UFO Controversy in America*, Signet, 1976

Carl Jung, *Flying Saucers*, Routledge, 1959, 1977

Donald Keyhoe, *Aliens from Space*, Panther, 1975

Peter Kolosimo, *Not of this World*, Sphere, 1971

Alan and Sally Landsburg, *The Outer Space Connection*, Corgi, 1975

Alan Landsburg, *In Search of Extraterrestrials*, Corgi, 1977

Desmond Leslie and George Adamski, *Flying Saucers Have Landed*, Spearman, 1970; Futura, 1977

D. H. Menzel and E. H. Taves, *The UFO Enigma*, Doubleday, 1977

Ian Ridpath, *Worlds Beyond*, Wildwood House, 1975

Ian Ridpath, *Signs of Life*, Kestrel, 1977; Peacock (Penguin), 1977

Carl Sagan, *The Cosmic Connection*, Coronet, 1975

Carl Sagan and Thornton Page, *UFOs: A Scientific Debate*, Norton, 1974

Ronald Story, *The Space-Gods Revealed*, New English Library, 1976

Leonard Stringfield, *Situation Red, the UFO Siege!*, Doubleday, 1977

R. K. G. Temple, *Sirius Mystery*, Sidgwick and Jackson, 1976; Futura, 1977

Brinsley Trench, *Flying Saucer Story*, Spearman, 1966; Tandem, 1973

Jacques Vallée, *UFOs, The Psychic Solution*, Panther, 1977